Praise for

APPLE PIE WITH LUCY

"We all learn our most significant lessons from stories. I hope you will let Melissa share this message with you through a story of a young woman and the wisdom she gains from her grandmother. Have a great read and a great life."

Jim Stovall

Emmy Award winner and

Bestselling author of *The Ultimate Gift*

www.JimStovall.com

"Living a life of significance does not just happen to us. We must consistently overcome and purposefully commit to ourselves and our dreams. Allow Melissa's book to support you in doing both."

Janine Shepherd

Internationally requested speaker and

Bestselling author of *Never Tell Me Never*

www.JanineShepherd.com

APPLE PIE WITH LUCY

a STORY of ONE WOMAN'S SEARCH for SIGNIFICANCE

MELISSA AIMEE HAUPT

APPLE PIE WITH LUCY
Livin' Your Dreams Publishing
Printed in the United States of America
First Edition, 2011
All rights reserved

Cover designed by: Melissa Linden, Sea Saw Marketing

ISBN 13: 9780615476889
ISBN 10: 0615476880

This book is dedicated to the one person who inspires me to be my best. My husband and greatest supporter, Tom Haupt.

Acknowledgements

There are so many people in my life who have made a difference and have added to the chances of this book even being an idea, let alone an actual complete and published book.

The first acknowledgement goes to God. In 2009 I kept getting a download from Him. Something about "Who you are is already enough" as a concept of a book. To which I would reply... "A book? Are you talking to me?". It wasn't that long ago that I would have even contemplated the thought of writing a book. It wasn't ever one of my dreams until 2009.

My journey in life is not too dissimilar to Sophie. It was through the personal development work at Klemmer and Associates that I was blessed in finding myself again. And I found the woman I was born to be. I found my authentic self. Thank you Klemmer and Associates for the gift. A special thanks to Brian Klemmer, founder of Klemmer and Associates, who passed away just five days before I wrote this. Because you chose to live a life of significance, I got to choose to be who I am today. Thank you. I am forever grateful. I will see you in heaven sir.

The greatest support person I have in my life is without a doubt, my husband. Tom Haupt, to whom this book is dedicated, is not only the love of my life, but the person who believes in me the most. He doesn't let my 'stories' get the better of me and loves me through to the finish line every time. Tom, you make me want to be a better person. Life with you in it is everything I could ever dream of and more. Thank you sweetheart.

Saying thank you to my parents, Darryl and Sharon Williams and my brothers, Timothy, Jonathan and Matthew, will never be enough to express my love and thanks to each of you. Thank you for being incredible.

Daniela Iacovella, you are the most special friend I have. You are such a joy in my life. Thank you for your pom poms and high kicks when you cheered me on from the side lines to get this book complete. Especially on the days when I said things like. "I wonder if anyone will even like it" or "I hope it's okay". You are far more spectacular than you know. I love you girl.

Lory Muirhead and Janine Finney who I have such love and respect for. It has been so great to be with you both on this journey together. Thank you for the times we have made magic together with our brain storming. I look forward to many more moments together.

Thank you to all my friends, who are like family, from my Klemmer and Associates journey. Those of you who I have met at each of the seminars. We have laughed many laughs together and shed just as many tears. Thank you for loving me for who I am. Some of you have experienced more of me than anyone in my life. Special thanks also to some of the facilitators at Klemmer and Associates. To my first facilitator, Diane Beinschroth. You sowed seeds in my mind and heart that I am forever thankful for. Thank you beautiful lady. Kimberly Zink, John Edwards and Scott Pullan. You spoke into my life time and time again, whenever I was brave enough to step into the room for *Advanced Leadership* and tear away another onion layer. You are all angels from heaven. Thank you, thank you, thank you. Also to Janet Henze and Centa Terry. Thanks for letting me play again. I am grateful you chose to see my greatness and trust I would show up the second time. It was a pinnacle moment in my life.

Lastly, to all the women in the world who are willing to take themselves on and be who they are purposed to be. You inspire me constantly.

Contents

1

It's Just Too Much

As I woke from a deep sleep there was a pang of disappointment that punched my stomach hard. I pulled the sheets over my head and cradled myself into a fetal position, begging for it all to be different. I didn't want to do life today. I had too many regrets of things done and not done.

This isn't foreign for me. I often wake like this, with the constant nagging that I'm not entirely happy and don't feel quite complete. That there's something missing. Each time, primarily from the guilt of feeling like this, I proceed to reason with myself... 'things aren't *that* bad... besides, there are people out there who have it much worse. I really should be happy with what I have'. For the most part I am, but I just can't shake these feelings. They tend to be their strongest when I first wake or when John, my husband, is away and I'm all alone again in this house, in this world.

Those who don't know me, or even those who do, most likely think I am happy and have it pretty good. At least that's what I figure it looks like, certainly hope it looks like. After all, I have a fairly good relationship with John, terrific friends and until the kids came, had a good job in a great industry. John has a great paying career and he seems happy. We have family vacations, a big house and drive nice cars. We have the usual 'white picket fence with two point five kids and a dog'. Actually, there's no dog - I am not an 'animal person'. And we have three kids. But you get the picture.

Maybe it was better when I was *pretending* everything was great. I think I even convinced myself I was happy and everything was just fine. I guess I just didn't let myself get real honest. If I did, I think I might open pandoras box and God only knows what we might find in there!

It's Just Too Much

I lifted my head off the pillow just enough to take a peak at John's alarm clock which he uses to blast himself out of bed each morning for work. Its little red numbers indicated it was ten past nine. I had slept heavy for the last hour, since returning to my haven, after seeing John and the kids off for the day. It was the first day of school break and the kids wanted to go to the zoo. I had just bought *Madagascar* on dvd for them and our youngest, Lily, had being doing her best to convince her bother David, our middle child, he would see a hippopotamus today. I had agreed I would meet up with them for hot chocolate in the afternoon. I needed to give myself some time today.

The sun poked it's way through the break in the curtain and stung my eyes. I wanted more sleep and the sun was hindering my urge to keep my eyes shut and drift back to sleep where dreams would surely keep me from my misery. As I lay there awake, the sudden realization of being alone, even though I had wanted it this morning, intensified and reared its ugly head. What was it about being by myself that caused this intensity in my sadness?

Perhaps when I'm alone I am no longer distracted from my thoughts and feelings.

All the hurt was snaking slowly through my head and around my body, ensuring it paid special attention to tightening its grip around my heart. Threatening to torture me until I relinquished all of myself and succumbed, it slowly engulfed what was left of my hope and it seemed to give me no other option than to surrender what was left of me. Sometimes *that* felt like the best option. To succumb to it that is. To just surrender and let it win, and then maybe I would finally be free. I have thought about it plenty of times, but never could do it. The price my kids would pay was too high.

Why do I feel this way? What is wrong with me? Tears start spilling out of me and onto the pillow. It rose up into my throat and I grasped at the bed sheets. "It's too much! I can't deal with this anymore. What is wrong with me? God... please tell me... what's wrong with me? Why does life have to be like this? I can't do it anymore." Although I don't think I was *really* talking to God, I cried out in a desperate plea punching my pillow. Letting some of the hurt out gave me some relief.

After bouts of sobbing and wailing and asking why. Why me? Why the hurt? I finally did it. You know - prayed to God. For real this time. As if I was talking directly to him. It was a real cry for help. Leaving out the drama, I asked with all the seriousness I could muster. "God, please take away this hurt. Fill my heart with love and take this pain from inside of me. I want to feel whole again." And with that, the hurt vanished from my heart and mind. I suddenly felt for the first time a sense of hope and in that moment God had heard me. I felt whole again, like I had been enveloped in pure white love. I fell back asleep smiling.

)()()()()()(

"Is she awake Daddy?"

Who is that? Is that Lily? I tried to open my eyes but they were too heavy. *Where am I?*

I called out to John. *Why can't he hear me?*

"Not yet Lily. Hey Daniel, why don't you take your brother and sister to the cafe at the end of the hall and get something to eat. Here's some money."

Daniel, almost eleven, is the eldest of our three children. He's bright, well mannered and usually the life of the party. Lately he has become quite withdrawn. He asked me recently if there was something he had done wrong. After questioning what he meant he said, "to make you and Daddy fight all the time". Poor child. No child deserves to carry that burden. Of course I reassured him it wasn't his fault but somehow my answers didn't seem to satisfy him.

Why are all the kids and John in our bedroom? Somehow it didn't seem like I was in our bed. *What is going on here?*

"Oh! Hi Rebecca. How are you?"

"I'm good John. I'm so sorry. Are you okay? How are the kids? I got here as soon as I could. How is she?"

It's Just Too Much

"Thanks for coming in. She is doing alright, considering. Here have a seat."

Are they talking about me? Why am I okay, considering? Considering what? What's happening? Why can't anyone hear me? Panic started to set in.

"I just don't understand. It's not like her to drive when she has been out with the girls. Are you sure she was the one driving?"

"I guess so John. I left her and the others early. She wasn't drinking and so she must have opted to drive them all. I'm so sorry John... if only I'd stayed... none of this would have happened. You know I always look out for our Soph."

"I know Rebecca. No sense in blaming yourself. I just... I just..."

I could hear John start to cry. He didn't do that often and never in front of anyone else but me. *Oh God... what have I done? Was I in an accident? Oh! God... no!*

I started to panic. Did I hurt anyone else? *My legs? I can't feel my legs. Please God. I'll do anything to have my legs be okay.*

"John... I wish so many things for you right now. I wish we could just start yesterday all over again. I wish I could tell you everything will be fine. But all of it's just a wish. You know I'm here for you and the kids through all of this. Anything you need, you just ask."

"Thanks. Thanks Rebecca. You're a true friend to Sophie. The best she has." He paused for a moment. "Let me ask you something Rebecca. Did she say anything last night about her grandmother?"

"No. Not at all. At least not to me. Why do you ask?"

"Well, the only person she seems to be asking for, when she does speak, is her Grandma Lucy."

"She didn't mention anything to me. She hasn't been asking for you or the kids?"

"Nope. Not once."

2

Apple Pie with Lucy

"Hello Grandma Lucy," I said with a smile as the door opened and a rush of warmth came from inside her home. She had a fire place which warmed the whole house and made it feel cozy in winter. Lucy was in her late seventies and she was still independent and lived in the home she had lived since she was married. Her husband, my grandfather, passed away four years earlier. It was a sad time for us all when he passed. My mother was especially affected. They were very close.

My grandfather built their home after he came back from the war. The government gave all war veterans the chance to build or buy a house with VA loans upon their return. Although it's modest by today's standards it was a grand home when they first built it. One my grandmother says was the envy of all her girlfriends.

My grandparents have one of *those* love stories. You know the one. The one where he has to go off to war just weeks after they first start dating. Then, after three years and very few letters between them, just enough to keep their love alive, they marry immediately upon his return and they promptly start a family.

My grandfather, Jim, was a kind and gentle man who stood six feet three inches tall and was leaner than a telephone pole. He was softly spoken and admired by everyone he met. He was the kind of man who didn't have a harsh word to say about anyone. I loved sitting on his knee as a young child, listening to his stories.

"What a lovely surprise! I was wondering when you would come," she said as she embraced me with a hug. Her short spindly arms wrapping themselves around me.

Apple Pie with Lucy

"I can't stay for long though Lucy. I am about to see John and the kids." I shivered. "It's not getting any warmer, will winter ever leave my bones?" I complained.

"Yes. It is awfully cold for this time of the year. Come on in. I'm baking pie. Your favorite," she said as she almost danced into the kitchen which was at the back of the house. She was so vivacious for a woman her age. It brought an alive feeling into my body and in that very moment I felt like I could do anything. Be anything. This is how being around Lucy made me feel. Alive!

I shut the door behind me, flinging my Gucci handbag, last years birthday present to myself, over my shoulder. I followed my grandmother through the living room and into the kitchen. I could smell the aromas I grew to love when I was a child. Today it smelled rich of cinnamon and green apple.

Visiting with her always brought about a sense of 'okay-ness'. A sense of belonging. I was always amazed at how wise she was. A beautiful soul that exudes love. She wasn't necessarily *that* successful in her life. At least not by my standards. Although she spent a lot of time abroad, she lived a modest life raising a family. My grandmother, like myself, only had three children, which was uncommon for that generation. I wasn't sure if she couldn't have anymore and that's why she only had three. I'd never asked her, or anyone in the family for that matter, why that was.

She seemed to have a different way of seeing things than most women her own age. Almost as if she was born in the wrong generation. She had always been forward thinking since I'd been old enough to see it. There was a sense of old and new with her. *Old* in that she was so wise and *new* in that she was so young in spirit.

There was a closeness to this woman I adored. I always felt at peace when I would hear her words of wisdom and was surrounded by her peaceful manner. As if we were the one same person when we were together.

"Why the worry in those beautiful blue eyes of yours Soph?" my grandmother asked, as I sat on one of the high breakfast chairs and leaned on the counter to watch her cut the fresh apple pie she had just baked. "You know I can see straight into your heart. Tell me what your heart speaks as I dish you some pie."

Apple Pie with Lucy

I sighed. How is it my grandmother could tell in an instant what my husband couldn't from years of this heartache? Even when I ventured to share with him from time to time. I don't always seem to be able to articulate to him what I'm thinking or feeling, so he is often impatient with having to 'read my mind'. But yet Lucy could see my dismay in an instant. I really wished John understood me like my grandmother did.

"I have those feelings still Lucy. Especially when I first wake. I just feel like something is missing. Sometimes I actually have some exciting ideas about what I can do with my life and soon enough I find myself finding reasons why they won't work. Or why I am not... " I paused, looking for the right words, "...equipped, skilled enough. Or don't have the money to start anything."

My grandmother was watching me with all the attention in the world, hanging on my every word. I went on, feeling total acceptance from this beautiful, loving woman.

"The kids are all at school now and I am not getting any younger. I just have this feeling my life is not what I thought it would be and I'm not looking forward to going back to work. It's like there is something more for me in this world and somehow I just can't seem to figure it out. I don't like living here. It's always so cold. Lately John and I have been arguing more and more. It's just not what I want in my life..." *Oh! God... I feel like I'm such a whiner! Just stop talking Sophie.* I looked up from my keys I was still playing with and met my grandmother's kind eyes. She was smiling at me.

"Yep. I know *that* feeling," she said ever so matter of fact and without judgement and implied the question, what are you going to do about it?, all in one sweep.

"I don't know what I am going to do about it," I replied to the unasked question.

Lucy softly took my chin in her hand, "Soph," That's what my girlfriends called me too. It was like my grandmother was one of my girlfriends, only much wiser. "you really must hear this from love when I say this." She paused. "It's *you*! You don't know the treasures of your heart."

She kissed my forehead and left me sitting there as she went to the next room to turn up the music she had playing. "I love this song!" She danced elegantly out of the room, her spirits high.

I was stunned. My grandmother was always direct and told me just what she was thinking. But this time it was different. I looked out the window into the backyard which was edged with stark dead trees, that would later, in the spring, bounce back to life. *What does she mean... my treasures?! How is this advice?* I started to get mad now. *If I had the money and didn't have to spend all my time looking after the kids things would be different. I don't want to go back to work. But I want to do something with my life. If only John was more attentive to my needs. He doesn't even listen to me anymore. It's not my fault we live here that's for sure! It's not ME... it's lots of things... but it's not me! What does she even mean by that anyway... treasures of my heart?* I let out a sigh.

"Soph, are you open to joining me on an adventure?" Lucy asked as she walked back into the kitchen from turning up a Frank Sinatra song. My grandmother loved music. When she was young she dreamed of being a professional ballroom dancer. She would have been good too. I think I must take after her. I also love to dance.

"Adventure? What sort of adventure?" I asked, still fuming from her last comments.

She leaned on the kitchen counter and took my hands in hers. "I like to think of it as a quest. One that gives you the opportunity to free yourself from some of this heartache and start living the extraordinary life you deserve Sophie."

I still wasn't sure what she meant by 'quest'. "Yeah... I guess so." I said with a quizzed look on my face.

"Well, I don't want you to *guess so*. If you want some resolve in your life Soph, I want you to take what I am asking seriously," she said as she took a step back from the counter.

I sat up, giving the question more thought on what was a frightening cold March day and found an overwhelming desire to say yes to whatever adventure she was about to take me on. I've felt so unsure of who I am and what I want. I've been busy raising three kids and I wasn't even sure I remembered what my dreams and aspirations in life were. Almost as if a piece of me had gone missing each time I spent time running after grubby fingered children and changing diapers.

"I guess I'm already aware of how much time I don't have." I started. I knew it was an excuse. I didn't know why but something inside told me if I wanted more in my life, this was a stepping stone.

"Yes Lucy. I'm in," I said with a small sense of trepidation. I knew commitment was pretty high on the list of character traits for my grandmother.

"Perfect. We'll start on Monday. But for now, let's eat some pie before it gets cold." She turned and collected some plates from the cabinets one of my brothers remodeled a few years ago.

APPLE PIE WITH LUCY

3

The Quest

It's Monday and the day to meet my grandmother for the *quest* I'm about to embark. My grandmother was a great teacher growing up. Although I didn't see her much I learned more lessons from her than anyone else in my life.

I dropped Lily off with the nanny and made my way to the park to meet her. Our other kids were at John's mother's and stepfather's place in Florida for the remainder of the March school break.

Why on earth we are meeting in a park in mid March in Wisconsin is beyond me! I was hurrying to be sure I wouldn't be late. I was already pushing to be at the park

19

by nine. Grandma Lucy didn't tolerate people being late. 'It shows how little you care or respect the person you are late for. If you can be five minutes late, you can be five minutes early.' I could hear my grandmother giving me this advice as if she was sitting in the car with me. Of course, my mother is always late. I think she's still rebelling against my grandmother to this day. I changed lanes to get ahead of a car which was moving far too slow for my liking. "What are you doing? Driving Miss Daisy? Move already!" I was starting to raise my voice now. I was often frustrated and short-tempered and didn't like it when John pointed it out to me either. Besides, he was just as short-tempered.

My grandmother was already waiting for me by her own car when I tore into the parking lot. I slowed and parked in the lot next to her. Jumping out of my black SUV, I grabbed my handbag and tossed my keys inside. I took a quick discreet look at the illuminated numbers on my running watch. It read 8:59. I was safe. She handed me a cup of hot chocolate. She knows I don't like the taste of coffee. I must be the only adult on earth who goes to

The Quest

'coffee' with friends and never actually orders one. "Good morning Sophie."

"Hi Grandma Lucy." The cold hit my face and I cringed. *I hate the cold.* "Why are we meeting here, where it's cold?" I was already not excited about the quest. I was inspired the day I agreed. Since then I had a whole weekend to think about it and was wondering if I made the right choice. Maybe things are okay after all.

"How we do anything is how we do everything Soph," my grandmother said, not answering my question about the apparent poor choice of the meeting place. *Why must my grandmother always talk in bummer stickers?!* I was compelled to quit. To just get back in my car and organize to meet my girlfriends for lunch. Besides, my girlfriends helped me take my mind off things, at least for a moment.

"Come, let's walk. I want to show you something," Lucy said as she put her arm around my waist and took a sip of her hot tea. No doubt she could sense how agitated I was.

APPLE PIE WITH LUCY

The park was beautiful. It wasn't actually a park, more like a monastery. The grounds were beautifully manicured and there were lots of buildings dotted around the two acre parkland. *I bet this place is beautiful in the spring.*

We walked in silence until I asked the question that was playing on my mind. "Lucy, what did you mean when you said 'how we do anything is how we do everything'?" I was trying not to convey how completely unaware I was of what she was talking about.

Lucy slowed down and came to a stop outside a small building and looked at me with her kind, soft eyes. "How you sped into the parking lot with seconds to spare before you knew you would be late. You know I don't like people being late."

She paused for a moment and looked up at the building that stood before us. "With everything you undertake with this quest Soph, I want you to notice how you are doing what you are doing. It's not to notice *what* you are doing. But, *how* you are doing it." She looked at me nodding, willing me to understand the importance of what she was saying.

"So how I drove fast into the parking lot is supposed to imply *that* is how I do *everything*?" I asked with an inflection of frustration, confusion, and slight sarcasm.

Lucy didn't answer and instead motioned for me to enter the small building. "This is a meditation room. Well at least this is where I come to meditate... and pray." The room was an octagon shape and was warm and inviting as we stepped in, shutting the door to the cold morning which would surely await us once we were done.

It was so peaceful inside, almost another world in which one could find themselves escaping too. The room was not very big and had four steps that looped around the middle of the room covered in soft brown colored carpet. There were also lots of different sized pillows dotted around the room which was painted in warm earthy tones. *It even has a fireplace! I need a place like this at home.*

We both sat in silence, taking in the serenity. I watched my grandmother as she sat quietly, mesmerized by the flames of the fire in the fireplace. She looked so beautiful. Her hair, completely grey, as it had been since she was in her early fifties, was gently pinned back and a couple of soft pieces sat softly around her face. I only remember her with grey hair, and the old photos of when she was young don't show the true reflection of the brilliant chestnut brown color it once was.

My grandmother broke the silence. "Are you ready to hear about this quest Soph?"

I had a sudden sense of anxiety rush through my body. It was made up of uncertainty and excitement. I knew my grandmother would truly challenge me and it's just what I needed in my life right now. I needed something. Maybe this would be the thing to fix me.

"I am Grandma Lucy. Where do we start?" I replied.

"Let's start with the expectations of the quest," she said with a let's-get-down-to-business demeanor.

I took out my notebook and pen from my handbag and drew open to a new page.

"Actually, first let me tell you where I first heard about all this Soph and then I will tell you about the specifics." I sat back and relaxed, placing my notebook by my side. I loved the stories my grandmother told. They were never embellished and always left me pondering a lesson to be learned from them. They were often stories from her times spent overseas. If I thought about it, my grandmother was quite the pioneer. She did some things in her day that no other women would dare have done. What fabulous role models I have had in my life.

"It was when your mother was about twelve. I was in India with your grandfather. Actually, it was before he and your mother both joined me. I had gone over to set up and they were to join me in a few months time." My grandmother and grandfather had spent years back and forth between their home here in the states and India, Indonesia and parts of South East Asia. They had spent most of their lives as missionaries and they were away in other countries more than they were in their own homeland. In fact, although they didn't go as frequently in the later years of their life, they only stopped going about two years before my grandfather had passed away.

APPLE PIE WITH LUCY

"I was staying with an elderly couple in their seventies and they were looking after one of their granddaughters. One day I asked the young girl about the old notebook she always had with her. The girl spoke better english than her grandparents and took her time to explain its importance. It contained notes from her mother who died giving birth to her fifteen years earlier. The notes were meant to be turned into a book, only the woman died before she had written it. It was all in Nepali and so I didn't take much interest in it at first." She paused for a moment and repositioned herself amongst the pillows.

She continued. "Truth be told Soph, given the oppression of women in those countries of the time I doubt the book was ever really going to be published. While I was there I saw this notebook often. There was much discussion about it among the family and what appeared to be some heated arguments at times. The arguments I believe were about this young girl writing a book. I guess the oppression remained and that book was never written. At least not during the time I knew them," she said shaking her head.

The Quest

"I learned these notes were profound in nature as they were taken from wisdom passed down from a woman named Sharesca, who was a well respected figure within this small community and influenced many young women. While living in northern India this girl's mother spent a few years working before a husband was found for her and she married. She was largely impacted by Sharesca. She also worked with another woman. A woman we know as Mother Teresa." My grandmother paused and looked at me. I was on the edge of my seat with intrigue. Why had I never heard this story before?

"Wait... did you just say Mother Teresa?"

She continued. "Yes. Before working in Calcutta, Mother Teresa spent time near the Himalayan mountains for a few short years before she took her religious vows."

"Did you ever meet her?" I interjected. I was fascinated. I really didn't know a lot about Mother Teresa's work or life for that matter. But, I knew enough to respect and honor such a courageous and giving woman.

"No. She worked up in that area before she went to Calcutta. It was years before I was in India."

"Sorry for interrupting. Go on."

"That's okay. So over the years of traveling to and from India and spending time with this family, I translated the notes and used the principles in my own life. They have served me well and I want to share these principles to support you Soph. I only wished your mother was open to me having these conversations with you when you were young. May have saved you some heartache," she said with an undercurrent of disappointment. I know she felt some sadness for the years her and Grandpa Jim spent overseas, disconnected from their family. Focused instead on her work, her relationship with my mother was somewhat strained. My mom never really appreciated what my grandparents were doing overseas and she remained in America once she was old enough as they continued to travel back and forth.

I sensed her sadness. "Well Grandma Lucy, you have taught me many lessons in my life. You're always a rock for me to depend on. I am blessed to have you." I said softly, reaching out my hand to take my grandmothers. She

28

took my hand in hers and smiled. "Thank you Soph. That means a lot. Now, where were we?"

"You finished telling me where these principles came from. But what do you mean by *principles*?" I was excited about this quest now. To think this all had Mother Teresa in the mix. My heart skipped a beat.

"Yes. Principles." She regained her focus. "The quest is made up of a set of principles. There are seven in total. Let me also explain to you about the framework."

"Framework," I said precariously. I wasn't sure I understood what she was talking about but didn't want to sound foolish.

"The quest is the framework for applying the principles. The principles are the *what*, the framework is the *how*." My grandmother paused to see if I understood what she was explaining. I motioned for her to go on and she continued. "Just knowing the principles alone is simply information. Information without application is just that. Information. Information doesn't change your life. We are all too often drowning in information yet are thirsting for wisdom."

"So you are saying you could *tell* me about the principles but unless I apply them it will just be words without life? Without meaning." I asked.

My grandmother responded with a smile. "I have never heard something so eloquently put. Yes, when you *apply* the principles they come to life. They grow wings and take flight and so do you. When you apply these concepts they become *your* truth. *Your* wisdom."

"I get it. So, how do I apply the principles? What's the framework?" I was excited about hearing this. I knew my life needed something right now. The thought of me growing wings and taking flight made my heart sing. *There's hope after all.*

"Excellent question." She motioned for me to get my notebook. "The quest will last for seven days. So, we will meet every day for a week. Are you good to do that?"

"Absolutely! I would love that. Daniel and Joshua are in Florida for the remainder of the school break. So it's perfect!"

The Quest

"Remember how I said to watch for *how* you are going about this quest? Not *what* you are doing so much, but *how*?"

"Yes. How I do anything is how I do everything. I remember." I wasn't sure I really understood what my grandmother meant and was resting on the hope it would make more sense as I undertook the quest.

"I get that doing this quest for seven days has significance with setting up the framework. But what do I actually have to do over the seven days, apart from visiting with you? What will we be doing?" I never had much patience. It was just the way I was. Always had been.

"Great question. Let me explain what all that means." My grandmother took her time to collect her thoughts. She never spoke without first thinking. "Each day you will learn about a new principle. On each of those days you will be responsible for implementing the principle into your own life, unless directed otherwise. And you'll also journal every night. Always watching for *how* you went about those days of implementing the principle."

"When can I get started?"

31

She smiled. "Eager I see. I have always admired that about you Soph. You take after your mother... and your grandmother I suppose." She patted me on the knee and smiled. Her eyes smiled too. With deep creases around them which showed she was indeed in her seventies. "Today!" She added with great enthusiasm.

"Before you begin Sophie I want you to understand one thing."

"Yes Grandma Lucy. What is it?"

"In order for me to spend my time with you on this quest you *must* be sure to implement the principles and complete the journaling. You're not to miss one day. If you do, the deal is off and you may not continue on the quest. Understood?"

"Um. Yes. Yes of course." I stammered. I don't always finish things when I start them. *She knows me inside out. I guess she already figured that maybe this would be something else I might quit before it's done.*

My grandmother started to get up and pulled a large envelope from inside her jacket. I stood and helped her up.

The Quest

"What's that Grandma Lucy?" I asked trying to keep my excitement under control.

"When you are ready to get started, open this envelope. Inside you'll find a book. This book is filled with the principles taught to me all those years ago. All you must do is go ahead and do what it asks you to do. For the first principle, just go ahead and do the journaling part. Don't read ahead about it. We will look at all of that when we meet here tomorrow. Okay?" With that she handed me the envelope, kissed my forehead and left the room.

I sat back down and held the envelope in my hands for what seemed liked forever. It smelled just like my grandmother.

I decided to spend some more time in that room, my new found haven, where I felt at peace and a sense of belonging. Now would be a great time to get started. I couldn't see the value of opening it when I was at home, with the busyness which goes on there. Besides, I was excited about getting started.

"Mother Teresa. India. Wait until John hears of this!" I said out loud. I felt like a kid in candy store as I hurriedly opened the envelope to retrieve its contents.

4

The Principle of

Self-Discovery

"Before embarking on a journey, first one must know, not where their destination lay, but instead, where it is they are beginning."

"It is not who you are, but who you think you are that matters."

Inside the envelope was an old leather bound book. It was beautiful. Like nothing I had ever seen before. It was embossed with ancient symbols and words. I ran my fingers over the front cover as if I was embarking on a journey that would transport me to another place or time. I opened the book to its first page which read:

To the woman who holds this book,

You have received this book because you are looking to fill an emptiness which consumes you. You are open to seeking more about what it is you want from life. You long for it. You wish to understand clearly your purpose and the way in which you can implement that purpose in your life.

It's like this book is talking directly to me. Only I don't think I seek to know my purpose. I guess I want to figure out what to do next with my life... but I don't think of it as my purpose.

Filled with absolute curiosity and wonder I returned my attention back to the book which read:

> **You are about to undergo a quest for seven days. You will discover seven principles which have helped other women, just like you, to embrace their uncertainty about themselves and their futures. Each day you will embrace each principle and implement it into your own life so it transforms you. Every day you will journal on the experience of implementing the principles. Journaling allows you to bring forth your deeper thoughts and get connected to who you really are.**
>
> **At times you will find yourself not wanting to do what is asked of you. You will sometimes find yourself forgetting, or**

finding something that is more important. This is your mind looking to keep you from growth. It is addicted to status quo. It does not like change. I challenge you to remain committed to this quest and notice how you are undertaking it. Ask yourself why you think the thoughts you think, feel the feelings you feel and act the way you act. Asking great questions will allow your higher level of thinking to bring about great answers. You will amaze yourself at the intelligence you posses of who you really are, of what you want and who you want to be.

Instructions for the quest:

* *You must commit to implementing each principle on the day in which you learned about it.*

* *You must commit to journaling each night.*

The Principle of Self-Discovery

The Principle of Self-Discovery
Day 1

Once you can identify with who you think you are you can then start to make progress toward knowing who you really are.

When you do not know who you are you risk the chance of becoming like someone else. Like those who you surround yourselves with. Like those who you admire. However, in life it empowers you to just be you. To be yourself.

As you begin this journey take a moment to understand where it is you begin. Do so with the following exercise:

Spend some time to answer the following: Who am I?

Take a moment to write about who it is you think best describes who you are. Simply write without concern of what comes out. Nothing is right nor wrong with what spills from your head and your heart onto your paper. Simply answer: Who am I? Not what others think of you or who others think you are. Not who you aspire to be. Nor who you wish you were. As you write let the question be asked in your mind over and over again, Who am I? Who am I? Who am I?

Seems easy enough. I took out my favorite pen and began to answer in the journal which was accompanying the book of principles. It too was leather bound and beautifully embossed with the word *Journal*.

At first I was writing about everything I wanted to believe about myself. The things I once *did* believe about myself. As I progressed and spent time with this question rolling around in my head I suddenly realized something very significant.

"I don't know who I am," I said in a whisper. A tear rolling down my face. Or at least the words I used to describe myself seemed detached from me. They were just words. I didn't feel a connection with them. I didn't feel like I owned them. *How is this so? How is it that I can be thirty-six years old and be so disconnected from myself?* I wiped the tears from my face and looked around the room hoping no one had entered and was standing there watching me cry. *And what the hell is going on with all these tears?!*

)(-)(-)(-)(-)(-)(

It was Tuesday, the second day of the quest and I was due to meet my grandmother in the afternoon. I had so many questions for her and was also a little nervous. I didn't feel like I did a very good job with the quest so far and I had only completed the first day.

I arrived at our meeting place and again I'm there just moments before being late. All day I've been trying to notice *how* I've been doing things. I've noticed I rush a lot and am in a constant heightened response to get things done quickly. I'm not sure what it means once I have noticed it. I stored the thought as a question to ask my grandmother.

Grandma Lucy didn't show any surprise response to my reflections of the exercise I started yesterday in the meditation room and continued at home, after dinner last night.

"The thing is Soph, we can spend our whole lives not really knowing who we are, not knowing what our strengths are, what our purpose is or what our hopes and dreams are." She paused and looked at me before she asked seriously, "What is it you are afraid you'll find Soph?"

I looked up and knew just what my grandmother meant by the question. I didn't want to go there though. To get that vulnerable with her, with myself.

The Principle of Self-Discovery

She touched my hand letting me know it was okay. That I was safe to share my thoughts and feelings.

"I'm scared to know who I *really* am." I couldn't believe I was even able to articulate that. *I guess spending time in reflection really does work.* I was on the verge of tears and knew if I opened the flood gates they would flow like the water at Niagara Falls. Hard and fast with no end in sight.

"What are you *most* afraid of discovering?" Grandma Lucy asked.

I wondered if my grandmother somehow knew the secrets I kept about the things I had done, the mistakes I had made. The ones no one knew about, not even most of my friends. Even the one where I had an abortion. That was the one I was most ashamed about. The one that seemed to haunt me the most. I'd stopped keeping track of how old the child would be. I had managed to push down the feelings and now as time went on the disappointment and guilt in myself had subsided, yet never really left. It was one of the darkest times in my life.

My grandmother continued, not concerned I had not answered her question. "Instead of taking time to seek our truth, we live life running away from ourselves and we push down our feelings. We live a life that is only surface in thought and feeling. We even hide behind our roles as a mother and wife, our jobs." She paused for a moment waiting to see if I was following her thought process.

"Yeah, I can see how I do that. When I was journaling on the same question, 'Who am I?', over and over, by the time I finished journaling last night I realized something more than all of that though. As much as I'm ashamed about what I've done, all the mistakes I have made and all the people I have hurt... I think I'm also afraid of how... *great* I could be. Does that seem obnoxious? I mean... I don't want to sound like I think I'm all that and a bag of chips.

"It's just seems like a lot of pressure. What if I really did know what my purpose was and it was something really huge? What if I'm meant to be the next Oprah? That's a scary thought," I said. There was something about Oprah I delighted in. I thought of her as a seemingly authentic woman with a tremendous amount of influence for good. I didn't really think for a minute that was my purpose. It just seemed like the biggest thing I could think of being in the moment. I still didn't really know what my purpose was. Or if any of us even have one for that matter.

"I agree with you Soph. I believe we are more afraid of just how much talent we have than how incapable we are. It took me a very long time before I realized that." She looked at me before taking a sip of her hot tea she bought at Starbucks on her way over.

"Then why do I think I'm incapable sometimes? I think I'm a confident person and I do think I'm very capable of a lot of things. However, I let the things I have not been so great at affect my confidence. Why is it that I don't always see spectacular when I look in the mirror? Why don't most women?" I was saddened at this point. Not just by my own feelings about myself, but for the other women I knew and didn't know. All the heartache that they feel. *Or am I alone with these feelings? I know there are a lot of women who don't like certain aspects of their bodies, however maybe I'm the only one who thinks like this. I feel so alone in all of this. I have never shared any of this with anyone, always afraid that I'm the only crazy person. But, maybe there are other women who feel just like I do!*

"They are some really great questions. Let's start with you. Why do *you* have these thoughts and feelings about yourself? Why do *you* choose to believe you're not capable, rather than believing the deeper truth that who you are is fabulous?" She asked.

I sat up and wished I could avoid her questions. I looked at a painting which hung on the wall in front of me. It was a painting of a waterfall amongst the most beautiful of green vegetation. I wondered where it was and realized I was allowing myself to be distracted. I *was* avoiding the question.

I brought my attention back and decided it was time to really find out what was going on deep down. "Why do I think I choose to believe who I am is not enough instead of believing who I am is fabulous?" I repeated the question out loud hoping it would help me to find the answer. It was like my mind was blank.

The Principle of Self-Discovery

"Let me explain two very important aspects to the way we all think. Not just you, but every person who was ever birthed into this world. Even Oprah," she said smiling at me. "What I'm about to share with you next Soph is one of the fundamental aspects of not only this quest but of what has made my life so much more shall I say... easy to be in control." She paused for a moment allowing me to hear what she was about to share. "You ready for it?" she asked. I nodded wishing my grandmother would hurry and reveal her thoughts already. She drew a deep breath and relaxed herself into the cushions which rested against the step she was sitting on and spoke. "*Every* feeling you have and *every* action you display in your life is created from a thought."

I looked at my grandmother, expecting her to say something more. To say something more profound. But she didn't. She just sat there, looking at me with those beautiful blue grey eyes. No wonder her grandfather had fallen in love with her. Those eyes could melt butter.

"Wait... that's it?" I finally said with obvious confusion and frustration. How could this be one of the secrets to my grandmother's deliciously happy life? There had to be something more than this. What has this got to do with the first principle anyway? The first principle is self-discovery. What do the thoughts I think have to do with self-discovery? Anyway, it seemed too simple. I was mad now. *I want some answers and this was NOT an answer.*

I think she could sense my frustration and responded to my question. "Knowing who you are or rather who you *think* you are is the most important foundation to start with. It is the key that will help you mould the other principles into your life." She paused for a moment, collecting her thoughts before she went on. "The ability to be constantly aware of who you *think* you are is the key." She stopped to make sure I was still tracking. I gestured for her to go on.

"Here's the second important piece to all this. When you understand that the thoughts you have directly and indirectly affect your feelings and actions, then you can better influence the outcome of your life.

"The challenge is our thoughts, feelings, and actions are so intertwined it can be difficult to identify the one causing the other to take effect. We are so complex in our wiring it almost appears as if all three are happening at once. In some ways this is true. We are often thinking, feeling and acting all at the same time, however, it is not always about the one and same thing. We could be *thinking* about what we will be having for dinner, while *feeling* upset that we didn't get the job we applied for, while we are helping our kids with their homework - which is an *action*. No wonder life can be exhausting!"

"So what you are saying is, my thoughts are the reason why I *feel* and *act* the way I do." I asked rhetorically. "When I feel so sad or... flat, about where my life is at and what I'm doing with it, it's because of the way I *think*?" I asked looking at my grandmother who was slowly nodding and smiling at me.

"Wait Grandma Lucy... I don't think about being sad or disappointed in my life, I just am. I just wake up feeling that way." I liked to be right and knew I wiggled my way out of taking any sort of blame this time. I stopped and wondered if this was an example of what my grandmother asked me to notice during the quest. *I might want to notice how I like to be right and not like to be blamed for things.* I decided I would store that thought away for later. Right now I wanted to make sense of this thought-feeling-action thing.

"That's a great point Soph. You're right about some of what you just said," my grandmother remarked.

"Let me explain. Be sure you stay with me on this. I'm going to be using terms you've probably never heard before. Let's continue to use your example about how you feel when you first wake. Now we've established you feel an emotion, like feeling sad or *flat*, as a direct result to a thought you have, let's also look at this phenomena in a another way. There are two types of thoughts we have, conscious and unconscious, of which we have many of at any given time. I like to think of it like this. Our conscious thoughts are the ones where we think on purpose. Our unconscious thoughts, on the other hand, are the thoughts we have when we are not 'thinking'. Like when you drive somewhere you have driven dozens of times and one day you take that same drive and get out of the car and think 'did I stop at that stop sign back there?'. You drove with your subconscious mind doing all the work. You were relying on the memory of driving that same route day in day out." She looked at me as if to ask 'is this making sense?'.

I nodded. "I understand what you mean. I like the way you differentiated between them. To me it's like being awake with my conscious thoughts and being asleep with the unconscious ones. Is that what you mean?"

"Yes! That's a great way to put it. Because we have so many thoughts not all thoughts are going to lead to feelings and then to actions in that given moment. Some thoughts are compounded upon over time which then cause a set of emotions you feel, and then a set of actions you take. Our thoughts, feelings and actions are not always conscious. They are most often unconscious. Almost like we don't have control over them!"

"I have never thought about all of this before. I have never even *heard* of this stuff before. Why has no one ever told me?" I was overwhelmed. This was a lot to take in.

She leaned forward and spoke with a serious, almost disappointed tone. "Most people don't know about it Sophie." She paused for a moment and then continued. "We actually think using our subconscious mind most of the time. In fact, approximately nine times out of ten we're using our subconscious mind to live our life. Being on autopilot and using our past experiences and lessons learned to make most of our decisions." She sat back again and placed her empty cup down beside her.

"I understand the part when I wake and feel sad, it's not because I consciously thought *on purpose* about feeling that way. But you're telling me I *feel* the way I do because my subconscious mind is thinking things I don't even know about?" I was amazed. I felt relieved in some ways. "I used to feel like the way I felt and my lack of doing anything about my situation was my fault. I felt bad about feeling bad. No wonder I was a mess some days!" Tears started to well in my eyes. I remembered how I felt about my lack of confidence and also how empty I felt on the days when I just wasn't sure about what I wanted to do with my life.

I started to cry harder now and tears tumbled down my cheeks. Lucy motioned for me to move over to her. She wrapped her arms around me and held me in a loving embrace. It had been a while since I'd been held like this. It had been a while too since I'd let my emotions out in front of anyone else. It was calming and I felt at peace there in my grandmother's arms.

She started to speak again and I sat back up wiping my face pulling a tissue from my coat pocket. No doubt my mascara was running. "You will read about all of this today. But I wanted to meet with you before then so I could explain it all. Then, if you had any questions you could ask me. By the way, this first principle is the only one that is this complex."

"Thanks Grandma Lucy," I said, blowing my nose.

"When I was living in India all those years ago and learned of these principles from the notes scribed from the teachings of Sharesca, I learned something of tremendous value. A very important piece to all of this and I would like to share it with you. Are you okay to keep going with all of this Soph?" she asked patiently.

Nodding, I took a deep breath and exhaled with a sense of relief. It felt good to be free of some of the blame I had cast upon myself for so long. "I feel good actually

Lucy. I feel somewhat relieved. Like a weight has been lifted from my shoulders." I smiled and took out my journal which to this point I had not actually written in, except for my journaling. It was nice to be hearing all of Grandma Lucy's wisdom and allowing it to wash over me instead of recording her words in the form of notes.

She started again and I sat looking at her, drinking in her words. "Emotions are also a response to a standard or an expectation you have, that is either met or not met by you or someone else. Let me explain by using an example.

"Let's pretend you have a standard that when John hugs you, you make the hug mean he is showing you love. And let's pretend, when he comes home from work tonight he gives you a hug. That hug meets your expectation and then you, subconsciously, create sensations in your body you have labeled *I feel loved*. You then react to that emotion. It might be in the form of a smile. Or it might be a return of a hug.

"The story you just created might be, 'when I receive a hug, I feel loved and I then smile and hug back, hoping it will last forever'. For someone else the story could be, 'when I receive a hug, I feel awkward and then I frown and pull away, wishing they didn't do that'. The stories we create all throughout our lives are what makes up our storybook. This storybook is the source we draw from when we make decisions." Lucy paused for a moment collecting her thoughts.

"And that storybook is our subconscious mind, isn't it?!" I was understanding this. "I can draw from this storybook without having to consciously think about everything I do. That's a good thing! But I can see how it is a bad thing as well." I stalled for a moment, remembering my grandmother didn't like me using certain words when I was young. *Good* and *bad* were two of them. I continued, looking to reword what I just said. "You know what I mean. It's great that I don't have to *think* all day long about what I'm doing. But, it doesn't help me when my storybook has stories like 'I am not smart enough', for example."

"That's true Sophie. When your storybook is filled with stories that don't support your greatness, then it holds you back in life. Every day you're making decisions about things in your life without even being aware you're making them.

"You see, from our storybook, which we spend our lives filling with stories, we give ourselves labels to identify *who* we are. Or at least who we *think* we are."

Now it was all making sense. *That's why all of this is so important for understanding the first principle, self-discovery. It's about understanding who we think we are at a deeper level. Much deeper level. Looking at the stories and labels we have that we don't even know we have.*

"Everyday we spend time, at a subconscious level, feeding our identity. And Soph, it's how we identify ourselves that dictates our outcomes in life. The labels you give yourself will define the way in which you live. They will affect the people you associate with, the car you drive, the job you have, even who you marry. The things you are willing to try and the things you are not willing to try. Everything you do or don't do will be based on what expectations you have for yourself, based on these labels developed from those stories." She was always so quietly spoken and grounded. So wise.

The Principle of Self-Discovery

I sat back into the pillows and took one of them in my arms, resting my chin on top of it as I pondered what my grandmother just explained. *I have to get my head around this. I think I understand what she's saying.* "What you're saying is pretty much everything I do is a result of the way I think and I don't even control most of what I'm thinking?" I asked rhetorically. Talking things out loud really helped me sort this new concept. "And the labels I have given myself are all expectations I'm either meeting or not meeting in my life. And... so where did I get these labels... I mean stories?"

"Great question! Most of these stories you established when you were just a child. You learned them from your parents and teachers... me, your grandfather... from anyone who was an influence in your life. Then, over your lifetime you have been establishing evidence to support these stories you have. At a subconscious level you have spent your life looking to prove yourself right about these stories in your storybook and hence your labels," she said, looking to see I understood what she explained.

I sure did understand. I couldn't believe though it could really be true. "Wait! So you're telling me that if I have a story about myself that was established from when I was a child like, 'I'm not smart', I will go about my life looking for evidence to prove this label or story is true?!"

"That's exactly what happens Sophie. Every time we're told something or experiencing something we are assigning meaning to it. We're fitting our experiences into boxes so our subconscious can draw on the information when required. If we were to use your example of 'I'm not smart enough', your subconscious mind will look for *evidence* to support that label."

She paused for a moment, pursing her lips together before she added a final thought. "It's like our subconscious mind is like a robot... in that it has no decision making abilities."

I waited for her to go on but she didn't. We sat in silence for a while. *This is such basic human behavior, why don't we know about this stuff? Did I learn this in psychology at college?*

The Principle of Self-Discovery

Lucy broke the silence. "Each and every event that happens and has happened in our lives impacts on the think-feel-act phenomenon. The reason being that each time we experience something we make up a story about it. Let's take that same scenario of being hugged and look at it in a new environment. Let's imagine you arrive home in a bad mood. You've had one of *those* days. You receive the usual hug from John and you instantly think 'Get out of my way, can't you see I am in a hurry to use the bathroom?' and then all of a sudden you're feeling angry with him because he gave you a hug. It wasn't the hug that provided the response, it was the thoughts you possessed in that moment. Thoughts that may not have even been attached to that scenario. The thoughts could have been to do with something completely different. So in that moment you made up a story about the event and so did John. Either a new story or more evidence to support the stories you and John had previously made up.

"Wow! This is fascinating stuff." I thought about how angry John and I had been at each other lately. *I wonder what stories I have that could be impacting our relationship?* I figured it would be a good idea not to ask Lucy about it. I would just journal about it later.

"Did you want to ask me something Soph?" Lucy said interrupting my thoughts.

"Um... well... I was just wondering if when I am angry at John, which is a feeling, am I really angry at him or just angry about something else... or *somebody* else?" I asked tentatively.

"Well my dear Sophie... only you truly know the answer to those questions. All I can answer is... *maybe*." She smiled, shrugging her shoulders.

"Let me tell you something else that is very important and one of the greatest lessons I have learned from all of this." Lucy continued.

"Our thoughts, feelings and actions are not who we are. *You* are not the thoughts you have, not the feelings you feel or even your actions. You must be responsible for them and acknowledge they are an extension of the storybook you have established. However, they are not *who* you are." Lucy stopped and looked at me.

The Principle of Self-Discovery

"Really? But doesn't that sound like it could mean someone who killed someone can just say 'well, it wasn't my fault. It was because of the way my father brought me up' and then anyone can just get away with anything?"

"I did say we are to be responsible for our thoughts, feelings and actions. It's just that they are not *who* we are."

Lucy propped herself up on one of the pillows and continued. "Let's use the same example we previously used about coming home and getting angry at John when he wanted to hug you and you need to use the bathroom. If we use it to explore our labels would you say you are a *selfish* and *rude* person?"

"Well, if what you said is true and I'm not my thoughts, feelings or actions then the answer is definitely no."

"I guess it was an obvious question with an obvious answer." She said smiling at me.

I smiled back at her, waiting for her to go on.

"You're right. Remember, a thought, followed by a feeling turns into an action. Therefore, your actions are a reflection of the way you think and feel in *that* moment either directly related to that scenario or to something or someone entirely different. However, they're not a reflection of who you are. Here's the clue... it's only once you let your behaviour define who you are that creates the label. That is defined only by you. And those labels are still not who you are. Make sense?"

I nodded.

"One of the greatest analogies I learned from Sharesca's wisdom that explains this is, your shadow is an extension of you, but you are not your shadow. Great way to put it huh?"

"Yeah.. it sure is." I replied chewing on my bottom lip. *This makes sense... but how do I change the storybook?*

"You look confused about something." My Grandmother interrupted my obvious deep-in-thought moment.

"Yeah... I'm not sure about something." I started to say, slowly. I was not even sure how to ask the question.

Lucy waited for me to collect my thoughts.

"If we have this storybook with all of our stories that affect our feelings and actions, how can we change our

62

storybook? How can we change our labels? We can change them, right?" *I hope so. Otherwise I'm screwed!*

"We sure can Soph," Lucy said laughing at my look of worry written all over my face.

"Thank goodness. So how do we do that?"

"Did I mention anything yesterday about how we learn? Did I mention anything about repetition and emotional involvement?"

I shook my head. "Nope."

"Okay. Let me explain that. When we are at school our teachers give us plenty of opportunities to learn a concept through different mechanisms. The most common way is by reciting it over and over. All of it to cause repetition of the same subject matter so that we will retain the information. Make sense so far?"

"Like our multiplication. Got it."

"Yes, exactly. The other way we learn is by emotional involvement. This is the most effective way of learning something. What I mean by emotional involvement is when we experience something and we have an emotional response to that experience. When we experience something it becomes our truth."

"Yeah but what do you mean by that?"

"Let me give you an example."

"Good. Sometimes it makes more sense when you explain things with life examples." I added.

"Do you remember when you gave birth to Daniel? The first time you held him?"

I nodded, eyes wide open. "Yes. I will never forget that. It was a natural birth and so it was *very* painful. And holding him in my arms was the most amazing thing. He just looked so perfect." My whole body shifted from the memory of the pain to the love I felt for each of my three children.

"Let me ask you a question. Do you think if you were explaining your childbirth experience to a woman who had never given birth before, she would truly get *your* experience? And what that pain and then subsequent joy meant to you?"

The Principle of Self-Discovery

"No way. She couldn't possibly. Unless you have been through childbirth you couldn't possibly know how it feels. Nor ever be prepared for it!"

"Exactly! As much as you can prepare for it, nothing will ever prepare you enough. It's just something you're going to have to find out for yourself."

"Yep. And it didn't matter how many books I read. Anyway, it seemed like everyone had a different method of dealing with all of it. It was just confusing reading all those books in the end."

"I bet. And have you ever experienced a time where you wanted to explain an exciting or equally horrifying experience only to think to yourself, 'there is no way I can even be bothered to explain this, they just won't get it'? Almost as if it would be doing the experience an injustice by trying to relay the story?" Lucy asked.

I nodded. I knew just what she meant. *But how does this relate to my question?*

Lucy continued. "The events in our lives where we have an emotional experience creates a new wisdom or truth about that experience no one else will ever have. It is

65

unique only to you. Just like your friends, possibly similar childbirth experience, will never be the same as yours. Why? Because it's *your* experience. Therefore it's *your* truth and it's part of *your* storybook.

"To answer your question... in order to change our labels is to change the stories in our storybook. To do that we must have new emotional experiences. But we will get to all that later in the quest. But does that makes sense at the moment?"

"I think so. If I have new experiences where I have emotional reactions to them I will be essentially changing the stories about myself. Like a new story about being smart enough?"

"That would be a great example. And the more experiences you have the more you will replace the ones you have right now that don't empower you in your life.

5

The Principle of Self-Acceptance

"Perfect is an unrealistic expectation of oneself."

"Mommy! I spilt the milk." My youngest daughter, Lily, cried out from the kitchen, waking me from my sleep.

My youngest of three children was growing up so fast. Soon, in the summer, there would be preparations to celebrate her fifth birthday. I had all my children, two boys and one girl, relatively close together. We hadn't planned it that way. It just kind of happened. Kind of sums up my life I guess. It *all* just kind of happened. I often find myself wondering, 'how did I get here?' This is not what I thought my life would be like. There was no planning for any of this. I just kind of rolled with it all, day in day out. Year in, year out.

"Coming sweetheart!" I called out as I threw my legs over the side of the bed and slipped on my slippers, reaching for my bathrobe which was hanging on the back of the bedroom door. I shivered from the cold and hugged my body to get back to the warmth I was enjoying in bed. March in Wisconsin was never a favorite month for me. In fact, none of the winter months were. I much preferred a warmer climate. We moved back to Wisconsin three years prior for John's work. He worked for a large accounting firm that transferred him when he took a promotion which included a company car, more money, and a lot less travel. That was the biggest bonus. I hated being apart so much when we lived in Florida. I really missed the beach and the sunshine though.

Instead we were here in the snow and the blizzards and the wind. Lately there have been the usual signs of spring but today would be another day with snowfall according to last night's weather forecast. Over five inches they are expecting. The wind lashed hard forcing the tree branches to whip the side of the house with a loud crack. *When is John ever going to trim that tree?*

My husband of nine years handed me some paper towel as I moved toward the kitchen to attend to a daily spilled cereal and milk fiasco, compliments of Lily as she insists on fixing her own breakfast. She is extremely determined to do things by herself.

"I have to get to work. Are you good to clean this up?" And with that John was off out the door with his briefcase in one hand and a bagel in the other.

"I guess so." I mumbled sarcastically under my breath, feeling the frustration of the love lost between us.

I often wonder if maybe we would be better off apart. But it's not like things are *that* bad. There I go again. Constantly convincing myself things could be worse. I do it a lot you know. It's just things really aren't *that* bad. They just aren't *that* great either. I always imagined being in a fabulous relationship where I was happy. This one is not and I am miserable.

We stay, I think, for the kids. They are still so young and I'm afraid of the impact it would have on them. John's parents divorced when he was seven years old and he took it hard. Although maybe it was better that way. His Dad used to drink a lot and his parents constantly fought. But, he says he missed his Dad growing up and rarely saw him. I know he doesn't want that for our kids.

So, for the kids, we stay. In a marriage that could be better but isn't that bad.

)()()()()()(

Grandma Lucy and I were meeting back again at the 'school for saving me from myself' and thankfully I was starting to feel a little different. The journaling has definitely helped. I was glad Lucy explained the first principle to me because I don't think it would have made *any* sense to me otherwise. But there was a part of all this which was overwhelming me.

The Principle of Self-Acceptance

I decided I needed to talk about my overwhelm. "Lucy?"

"Yes Sophie," she responded touching my knee. She could sense my hesitancy.

"Well... I'm not sure how to ask this. So I figure I'll just come out and say it. Now that I'm noticing all these thoughts, feelings and actions I kind of feel even worse about myself. I feel really overwhelmed about it. I mean, I am *really* screwed up! I realized last night just how much I'm probably screwing up my kids too!" *There... I've said it. I feel like a screw up! I don't know if I have ever actually told anyone that before. I guess I always held this 'I'm okay' front so people didn't find out who I really am. I don't think I've ever been able to articulate that either. Where was all this clarity coming from?*

"Even if you did actually ask a question... I don't have an answer for you right now Soph. But, I think when we talk today about the next principle, self-acceptance, it will help answer some of your concerns. I hope you read all about it before we met."

I nodded. "Yep. I sure did. I'm glad we are going to talk about it though because reading about it didn't really help too much."

"Okay. Before we get onto that, let me add a couple of things about the principle of self-discovery. Remember we talked yesterday about how you are not who you think you are, no matter what it is you think? Well, most of who you think you are, your body and even your personality, are all just a part of the 'costume' you have while you are here."

She looked at me to see I was on track with her, then continued. "This is not who you are and who you are all at the same time."

"Yes. I remember reading about that too. There are three parts to who we are. Our body, our mind and the third is our soul. Is that right?"

"Yes. Who God created us to be in a physical sense, our body and our mind, is essentially a costume and one we contribute to dramatically. Granted this is not *who* we are, it helps us identify ourselves as the earthly existence in which our soul resides. Essentially though, who we are is our soul."

"Yes. But it is essential we help create the best costume we have to support our purpose here on earth." I remembered this part well. I was just hoping I hadn't screwed up my costume so badly I needed to ask God for a trade in.

Lucy added to my thoughts. "Granted a lot of this is predesigned - we don't get to choose our body type or our eye and hair color. But at some level we still get to choose how we *show up*. And I am not just talking about the latest Gucci shoes we are wearing either or how *in shape* we are. The not so obvious I'm referring to is the way we get to contribute to our mind - our thinking and therefore the way we feel and act."

I leaned back against the step I was sitting on, full of thoughts. I had given a lot of needless energy to having a lot of *stuff* and I couldn't help but wonder why I hadn't given much in way of contribution to my mind over the years. "I have never thought of the importance of most of this Lucy. I mean I'm always positive and read lots of positive kinds of books. But, I don't feel as if it has really contributed to my mind. At least not in the way you are talking about."

"Before yesterday you were not even aware you have two parts to your mind. I guess the difference is, now you're aware, you can contribute *on purpose*."

She made a good point. "Well, I am certainly glad I'm learning all of this from you Grandma Lucy. I have no excuses now," I said smiling at her.

She returned a smile and one of her nope-you-sure-can't looks. "Can I ask you a direct question Sophie? With the promise you will give me a direct and honest answer?"

"Um.. Yes. I suppose so. Do I really have a choice?"

"One always has a choice Soph."

"Then yes. Ask away." I swallowed hard. *What the heck is she going to ask me? Oh! God... please don't have her ask me something I'll have to lie about.* There are certain things I have never told anyone. I certainly am not going start now by telling my *grandmother*. She's very loving, but there are certain things I would be afraid of even her knowing about. Of *anyone* knowing about.

The Principle of Self-Acceptance

"Do you believe you're broken Sophie and need fixing?"

I looked down at my feet and wished the floor would swallow me up. I thought about her question and how I *really* did feel about myself. I slowly answered her question, to which she obviously knew the answer. "Yeah. I guess I do Lucy. I feel like I have done some things I can't ever undo and I just wish I could start again and do it all over. The next time without making so many mistakes." I sighed and looked up at the painting hanging on the wall. The same one which had probably been hanging there since the building had been built. The one I looked at every time I couldn't bear to look at my grandmother for fear of crying.

My grandmother spoke gently. "You are not alone in all of these feelings Soph. I bet your girlfriends feel like this too. I know I have felt like that in my life." She paused, thinking for a moment.

"The great thing is, we always have the chance to create a new life. One that looks entirely different from our past. Every day we get to choose. But please know this...

you are not broken and certainly don't need fixing." She paused and waited until I acknowledged I heard what she said. "I want to talk to you about the next principle, self-acceptance. Are you okay to keep going?"

I nodded. I was afraid if I opened my mouth it would somehow indicate to my brain it was time to start the waterworks. Any slight movement just might be the *thing* to set it off. *Why is it I'm crying so much lately?*

"Would you say I am an empowered woman Sophie?" Lucy asked without the slightest amount of ego.

I answered her with admiration. "Yes. Absolutely." She not only seemed empowered, she was also empowering to so many others. Especially to other women.

"Sharesca mentions in her notes, to be an empowered woman means owning all of who you are. The good, bad and the ugly. It's not about waiting until you have it all together before you start seeing yourself as fabulous. That's like waiting for all the traffic lights to turn green before you will start your car in the morning. It's about accepting yourself for who you are *now*. Hoping you will one day 'be enough' will never bring you happiness.

The Principle of Self-Acceptance

Nor will it support you in living out your God-given purpose."

"Yeah... well... I don't do *that*. I'm just confused about *what* to do. I really don't have a clue what I'm meant to be doing. And besides, I don't exactly have the money to start my own business and so I guess I will go back to work. But, I don't really want to do that." I realized I was rambling and so I stopped and looked at Lucy. She was looking at me with one of those are-you-finished-with-your-BS looks.

Okay time to get honest. I realized a long time ago I *do* wait for all the traffic lights to turn green. For all conditions to be perfect before I do anything. "Ugh! I really do that don't I Grandma Lucy? I feel like I have to wait until I know enough, until I have my life figured out before I can do what I want to do." *Oh! no... I wish I could take that back. I don't want to discuss with her what I want to do. Not yet. I hope she doesn't ask me anything.*

"Yes. And do you feel like you don't see yourself as being *fabulous* until you have it all together?" She didn't ask about my ideas for what I want to do in life. I was safe for now. I actually have an idea of what I want to do. I just have so little idea about how it could look it seems so impossible to achieve.

"Well... I feel like I have to be... to be..." I was struggling to get it out. "I feel like I'm not good enough on so many levels. Besides, if I think I am fabulous or amazing then other people will think I'm full of myself. No one likes someone like that."

"Really? I think I'm amazing. Do you think I am full of myself?"

"Well... um... no. Of course I don't think you are full of yourself. But you *are* amazing. You don't just *think* you are. You just are! There's a difference."

"I disagree. I can see what you are getting at so let me explain it like this. Perhaps the people you are referring to, actually don't think that way about themselves at all. That's why they have to *act* that way. It's their act. It is a defense mechanism so people around them won't really know they don't think of themselves as amazing at all. Does that make sense?"

The Principle of Self-Acceptance

She continued with her next thought without waiting for an answer. "For those people who believe who they are is enough are the ones who don't need to *act* like they are enough. They are just going about their life, simply *being enough*."

"Yeah, but isn't it because they *are* enough? Like they have PhD's and amazing careers and they are naturally beautiful and have amazing husbands who cherish them." I felt like a thirteen year old with an awkward and inexperienced view on the world.

She smiled at me. The love that spills out of this woman is extraordinary. "Nope. In fact, because it's all about the way we think about ourselves, it actually works the other way round. The people who have all of what you mentioned earlier is because they think they are good enough first and *then* they go about doing and having all the things you were talking about. A person who believes they are smart enough is the one who would go ahead and apply to complete their PhD. Does that make sense?"

She paused for a moment. I could tell she had something to add. I waited for her to collect her thoughts before I asked the next burning question.

She continued. "And let me tell you this... no one person who walks this earth has it all together. Don't ever think that for a minute. What we see is *not* always the truth or the reality about something or someone. Did your mother ever tell you 'you don't know what goes on behind closed doors'?"

"Yes. But I never thought about the significance of it."

"It's very significant. Don't ever put people on pedestals thinking *they* have what it takes and so then you look to emulate them or don't even bother doing things in your own life because you don't 'measure up'. That's ridiculous! For a start, they are no more equipped, talented, skilled or gifted than you or I. And things are *never* as they seem. Besides, looking to be like someone else is the most disempowering thing one can ever do for themselves. You are better off being an average version of yourself than looking to be the best qualities of someone else. God made

80

you, you." She paused then added "And that's all I have to say about that!" She smiled and looked at me as if to say 'so there you have it!'.

I laughed. She was so passionate about this. "Do you think I do any of that Lucy? You know, put people on pedestals?"

"Don't look to other people to find your truth Soph. You know all the answers. You already have everything inside of you. Seek to find your own answers my child." I loved how she still called me 'my child'.

"Well, I guess... I mean... Yes. I do that. I'm *often* putting other people up on a pedestal. But, what about someone like Oprah? You don't think she has more talent than me? I mean she is so successful. She deserves to be on a pedestal."

"Yes. I agree she deserves to be *respected* for what she has accomplished, even admired. But, first answer me this. Do you think Oprah has fined tuned her skills as she has been doing what she has been doing for so long?"

"Yes. I guess the longer she has been doing her talk show she's become better and better."

"You better believe it! She has been doing her show for over twenty-five years now. You think she was always this good at what she does? Secondly, do you think she just got handed a contract to have her own show the moment she decided that's what she wanted to do?"

"I'm not sure. Probably not."

"However, what made Oprah different from other people around her in order to have both been offered the show and be as successful as she is now?"

It was all starting to make sense. "It wasn't because she was born 'Oprah' who was extraordinarily skilled, talented and more brilliant than the next person. It's because she had a different way of thinking about herself." A lightbulb went off in my head. "She believed she was good enough to do whatever it took to do for her to get her show."

"Now does that necessarily mean she has 'it all together'? Does it mean she is totally accepting of herself?"

"No. I guess not. Do you think she is?"

"What? Totally accepting of herself? Nope. I don't think anyone is. We all feel inadequate sometimes. It will always be like that. Besides, some people actually use their lack of not feeling adequate to prove to other people they are enough by overachieving. But, let's not get too sidetracked. Let me get back to self-acceptance. Unless you have any questions so far?"

"Nope. I'm all good."

"Okay. When it comes to the principle of self-acceptance it's important to remember fundamentally it's about accepting *all* of who you are. It's not about accepting the great things and looking to change the not-so-great-things about yourself.

"You see, when we are not accepting something about who we are, the way we act and so forth, it's because we are in judgement of ourselves. Judgement is simply a comparison between how we think something should be and how we think it is. Most of the time there is no truth to it. It's all made up based on our storybook. By accepting ourselves, and others, we are free of judgement." She paused.

I waited.

"You know what I think?" She pursed her lips thoughtfully. "I think the biggest challenge for you Soph, might be to realize, the more you think you need to change who you are the more you will struggle with the big, dark, gaping hole you have in your heart.

"It's also about forgiving yourself for the things you have done that you're not proud of. Remember, you are *not* your thoughts, feelings and actions, so forgive yourself and cut yourself some slack for the times in your life where you've had moments of acting out of your ego and not your soul. It doesn't matter what it is you have done, said or otherwise that you deserve to be keep beating yourself up about. You understand Soph?" She paused only for a moment before she delivered what was to be one of the most defining moments in my life. As if spoken from God's lips to my ears.

"The aim of the game we call life is to live as congruent with who we are authentically. The woman who God made *you* to be. The woman who is amazing, talented, gifted, unique, and qualified to live out the very purpose which was planted in your soul when you were birthed into this world. A purpose to solve a problem which exists in the world at the very moment in history in which you were destined to live."

I was overwhelmed with emotion at this point and my brain was on full alert to open the gates which would allow the river to break free and flow out of me. "Wow," I said quietly. It was all I could muster.

"It's all true Soph. Who you are is absolutely enough. Will you, in this very moment, be open to accepting that?"

I heard all of what my grandmother just said but her words seemed to come from somewhere else. It was as if they came from inside of me. My heart was filled with such love in this moment and as if on queue the tears started to flow. It was probably the first time I'd ever felt so loved for as long as I could remember. I didn't know where it was coming from, but it was consuming me from the bottom of my feet to the top of my head. I felt like there was hope in my life and everything would be okay. In that moment I had an overwhelming feeling I was no longer broken.

I looked out the window and realized the afternoon slipped by without me noticing. The partial sun which once graced the side of the building had disappeared and was instead marked by the gloom of a winters short day. I looked at my watch. It was almost five and I had to get to Lily. *Maybe John will have to pick her up. What has happened to the afternoon?*

Lucy noticed my sudden realization. "Do you need to head out or can you stay another few minutes?"

"I won't make it in time to collect Lily anyway. Let me make a call to John to be sure he can collect her," I said as I hurriedly hunted for my phone in my oversized handbag.

Lucy waited patiently and walked around the room looking at the paintings hanging on the walls while I called John.

"He's fine. He wasn't very happy about it. But he'll get her. So, where were we?" I stuffed my phone back in my bag and returned my attention to Lucy as she resumed her place by the fireplace.

The Principle of Self-Acceptance

"There is just one more thing before we meet again tomorrow," she said brushing at her pants and straightening her shirt.

"Yeah? What's that?"

"What's the one thing you discovered about yourself so far that is your biggest story so to speak?"

"Biggest story? What do you mean, my *biggest* story?"

"What's the one story in your storybook you think holds you back the most? Does that make sense?"

"Yeah... I think so." I said slowly thinking about some of the stories I discovered in the short time Lucy and I had been on this journey.

"That's okay. Take your time. First thought is usually always your best thought though."

"Well, in that case, the first thing I thought about was the fact that I don't think I am knowledgeable enough. I don't think I have all the qualities yet. I have to wait a little bit longer. You know... until I have success, then I can start doing some things."

"Start doing what things Sophie?"

APPLE PIE WITH LUCY

I chewed on my lip and looked down at the pillow I had resting on my lap. I wished I didn't have to tell her what I think I want to do with my life. I swallowed hard and took a deep breath in. I *did* want her to know. I just didn't want to sound stupid. Finally I spoke. "I want to inspire women somehow. I can see myself being a speaker or a trainer of some sort. Maybe do some workshops or something."

"And so you feel like you have to have some success before you can do that?" she asked.

"Yeah. I feel like... why would anyone listen to me if I haven't had any success yet. I mean... what do I have to say that could benefit other women?"

Lucy didn't respond and we both sat in silence for a while. I liked that Grandma Lucy didn't always have to give me advice. She was a great listener and I felt like sometimes I could figure things out when I talked out loud and she just listened. This time it was no different.

"So... I think I have figured it out. I think who I am is not enough. And so I have to wait until I am enough before I can inspire other women. That's my story. My story is *I'm not enough.* Wow! I can't believe it!" I don't know why I was so excited. I mean that story is holding me back and yet here I was, excited. I guess it was because I finally figured it out.

)(")(")(")(")(")(

It was eight at night and I still hadn't thought of a way in which I could implement the principle of self-acceptance into my life. I've likely been over thinking it.

Tired and feeling like my head could explode from everything I'd been learning over the past couple of days, I chose to write myself a letter about all the things I accept about myself. I figured I would do that and if it wasn't good enough I could always do something else that would be better. Then it hit me like a bolt of lightning from a dark and stormy night sky. I realized in that moment, I didn't even trust myself to implement the principle the 'right way'. But instead, maybe the way I thought of doing it was 'wrong' or 'not good enough'.

The realization was freeing and so I chose to write a letter of self-acceptance to myself.

6

The Principle of
New Stories

"We only ever live up to the expectations we have of ourselves or of those that we allow others to have of us."

"I am the master of my fate. I am the captain of my soul."
- Invictus. William Ernest Henley.

"Why are we meeting here Grandma?" I really have grown to love the haven we have been meeting at for the last couple of days of the quest.

"You'll see."

APPLE PIE WITH LUCY

I walked with Lucy. She obviously knew where to go.

Today we were meeting at a church. It had been a while since I'd been to church. Growing up my parents had gone most Sundays, so we went to Sunday school and then youth church. That was a *long* time ago. Since then, John and I have gone on and off over the years.

This church was modern and had lots of buildings dotted around. It was almost as big as a college campus. Kids were running around chasing each other playing 'Tag - You're it' on the grass which showed the affects of the winter it had been enduring. But the kids didn't seem to care. The buildings all had big signs posted telling us what each were used for. We walked past one which read 'Kids Club. Ages 3-5 years'. *How fun. I would love to own an establishment like this. I would have a school and university for women who hadn't finished school. It would be more of a practical approach. I would love to help them set up a business. It could be a business school. There I go again! More crazy ideas. UGH!*

The Principle of New Stories

"So, tell me what you have discovered about yourself in the last couple of days." Lucy asked as we walked slowly by another open area where some older kids were kicking around a soccer ball.

"So much really. It's hard to know where I would start. The last journaling about self-acceptance was great." I paused. I had learned so much. My head felt like a spinning top and I wasn't really sure what answers she was looking for.

She smiled. "Tell me all about that for starters."

"It was just nice I guess to notice so many things about myself yesterday. I can't believe we are only a couple of days into this, by the way. It feels like time is a little warped at the moment." I paused and watched the kids running after each other and thought about my own kids. There's something about the love a mother has for her children.

I continued. "It was kinda confronting yesterday to discover one of the reasons why I don't do anything with my ideas is because I don't think I'm good enough to do all of the things I've dreamed about doing. I didn't ever think about it consciously before. It's like I wasn't really aware of what I really thought about myself. Does that makes sense?"

"It sure does. And there are no surprises in what you have discovered Soph. You're not alone that's for sure. And even if you do believe or have stories you're confident... the biggest stories will always win. You can always tell which stories you are living in accordance with. Want to know how you can tell?"

"Yep. I sure would."

"You can always tell based on what you are doing or what you have in your life."

"What do you mean?" I asked confused.

"Whatever results you have in your life is a reflection of how you think. They are reflection of your biggest stories."

"That's why you asked me yesterday what's my biggest story."

"That's right. And to be honest I was very surprised you managed to identify it so quickly. I wasn't so fast to figure mine out. Maybe I was just stubborn. Your grandfather was not the only one who has accused me of that!" We both laughed.

"And there are so many that we have. Stories, that is." I added.

"Yes. Remember though too, you also have stories that aren't all bad. Stories that have gotten you to where you are today. With all the success you *have* had."

"Right. I don't want to forget those. So, what are we doing here Lucy?" I was anxious to know why we were meeting here.

"I have a surprise for you Sophie. But before we get to that, I want to discuss something with you which is very important in all this. You want to walk over to the Starbucks cafe and get a hot tea?"

"Sure." *There's a Starbucks here? This place is awesome! Not like church as I remember it.*

We found the Starbucks and I ordered a hot chocolate and a chocolate muffin. It was fat free so I figured, why not? Although, I am yet to be pee-my-pants excited about a fat free muffin.

After we got our order we found a nice quiet table in the corner and Grandma Lucy kicked off our daily ritual of learning. This guidance was just what I needed in my life right now. I was hungry for it. The next principle was 'new stories' and I was hoping my grandmother had some solutions for me.

"Before we look at the next principle, I want to talk to you about something else which wasn't included in the notes from Sharesca."

"Works for me."

Lucy took a sip of her chai tea and smiled.

"I want to set you up to win during these seven days we are together Sophie. In fact, in life, you want to always be setting yourself up to win. Things in life don't need to be so hard.

"Always look to play life to win in the most empowering way. Ask yourself, how can I empower myself and others in such a way that we win with fun and ease? Life is a precious game Soph. It comes and goes so quickly and before you know it you're whisked away.

The Principle of New Stories

"I want to first look at the premise of being empowered or disempowered."

As I sat there and listened I thought about how much she truly did live while she was busy raising a family all the while living on purpose. I don't think I ever thought about it before, but she really has made such a difference in this world.

"What I mean by being empowered is, something which is supporting or promoting your greatness. And therefore disempowered is something which is *not* supporting or promoting your greatness. It really is that simple I guess. But let me explain a little further.

"Being empowered puts you in a responsible state. I once heard that Tony Robbins guy say, being responsible is being response able. Meaning when you are in an empowered state you are better able to respond. An empowered state allows you to be focused on finding a new solution. Provides you with new understanding. You are more open to learning something new about yourself or a situation. It gives you the power to make decisions and moves you into action mode.

"When you are in a disempowered state it focuses you on the problem and even makes the problem bigger. You find yourself in an unresourceful state as you are simply problem focused, not solution focused. It puts you in the victim questioning of 'why me? Why does this always happen to me?'" She took another sip of her tea and so I took the opportunity to clarify what she was talking about.

"So what you are saying is, to be empowered is anything which is said or done or thought, which supports me in my greatness and makes me more responsible and able to respond to situations better?"

"Yes my child."

"But, what exactly do you mean by my *greatness*?"

"Excellent question! You are a star student miss Sophie."

"Thanks Lucy. It's been a long time since I have heard that. Come to think of it, I don't know if I ever heard that." I remarked half joking. I was a pretty good student at school. I just don't remember being a *star* student. I was too shy to raise my hand with the answer most of the time and too scared I would get it wrong.

"Your greatness, Soph, is all of who you are essentially. It's the essence of who you are. Or at least, it's who you were born to be. Before all the stories you added to your storybook that you have chosen to attach as labels to your identity, which disempowers you from living as the woman you essentially are. Remember I've said, you already posses all of the qualities you need to live out your God-give purpose? *That* is what your greatness is!"

I must admit, I was a little confused. I just didn't get how this was that profound. Isn't she just saying 'You're awesome! Rock on Sophie! High five!' and then tomorrow after the motivational hype, kind words and a pat on the back I go back to my life still with the stories about how I'm not *that* awesome after all?

"I'm kind of confused about how this is *that* profound Grandma Lucy. Sorry, I love your enthusiasm for how great you think I am. But I just don't get that it's that... I can't think of a better word... profound."

Lucy smiled at me and took a sip of her tea, thinking.

"Imagine Sophie you were born filled with unlimited potential, together with all the wonderful qualities including things like courage, compassion, and trust, as well as a mind to learn all the skills you would also need to live out your God-given purpose. Do you believe you would have everything you need to be empowered to live out that purpose?"

"Yeah. Of course."

"Well, I believe we are all born with this potential. However, we always have a choice. As we move through life we can either choose to be empowered and live authentically as we were created to be, or disempowered by living in accordance to our storybook."

"You really think I can just choose right now to be courageous, compassionate and whatever else you said?" I wasn't sure I was buying all of what Lucy was selling me.

"Absolutely! However, remember your subconscious mind is very powerful. That storybook you have been adding stories to is what you *think* is your truth.

The Principle of New Stories

You *think* you are not enough to be an inspiration to women. It's a constant choosing that must take place while you are *awake* in your life."

I sat there playing with my grande Starbucks coffee cup which now contained dregs of what was once a hot hot chocolate. *The solution to new stories is to just choose to believe that I am super-duper-fabulous?! Sounds like a stretch to me.*

"Is this about changing out our stories for better ones? Or something different? Because I thought we were going to talk about changing our stories later."

"Yes. You're right. I'm going to give you some ways in which you can develop new stories that are going to *empower* you in living authentically as God created you to be. I just wanted you to get how much potential you have and how important it is to be in constant empowerment in your life. And to be sure others around you are giving you that as well."

"Yeah... that's for sure! I have seen how some of my friends are not always very *empowering*. I don't call it that though. Some of them just seem to suck all my energy out of me. You really believe we are all born with that potential and we allow ourselves and others to slowly etch away at it, over time?"

"I really do," Lucy said assuredly.

"I've certainly never thought of it like that before. So does it mean we will take just as long to get back to how we were authentically made? Because, that would really suck. Sounds like too much work."

Lucy laughed. She was likely laughing at either my 'that would suck' comment or my 'sounds like too much work' comment. Or both.

"No. Thankfully. Sharesca was very implicit in her teachings about how our potential allowed us to instantly go back to our authentic self at any moment. And the more we practice the better we get at doing that. And of course, the more we develop new stories the easier it is too. Remember, one of the ways in which we created our stories was when we had an emotional experience or through repetition. We will look at this closer very soon."

I nodded.

The Principle of New Stories

Lucy looked at her watch. "You ready? Ready for that surprise now?"

I was immediately excited and anxious all at the same time. I loved surprises, but for some reason I felt a little concerned about what Grandma Lucy had up her sleeve.

We walked to a nearby building where dozens of women were standing around chatting as well as dozens more filing into what appeared to be an auditorium. We made our way to the entrance and stepped inside a large room with big screens and music playing. On one of the screens it read 'Women's Love Out Loud Conference'.

"Come down toward the front Sophie. I have VIP seats. I come here every year." I followed my grandmother and wished I was wearing something a little dressier. *I didn't straighten my hair this morning. I wish I'd known we were coming to this! Yes I know... I have a story about needing to look good.*

The journey to the front was a unique experience. My grandmother was greeted by many women and I even caught some of them pointing and whispering to each other,

103

"That's her. That's the woman I was telling you about." My grandmother sure seems to be famous around here. I started to think I didn't really know my Grandma Lucy as much as I thought.

The conference started. They opened with a talented singer with the most beautiful angelic voice. I have always wished I could move people emotionally with my singing. Come to think of it, I probably do move people emotionally with my singing - like the emotion someone gets from hearing fingernails on a chalk board. Singing is *not* something I was gifted in life!

There were guest speakers lined up for the day. The first speaker spoke about what she felt it meant to 'love out loud'. I was enjoying myself until Lucy leaned over and said "Are you ready to learn about how to develop new stories?"

Confused I asked, "Now? What do you mean? They are introducing the next speaker. You want to do it now? I would really like to stay and hear all the speakers."

With that I heard the unbearable, most unthinkable thing. I heard myself being introduced as the next speaker. I looked at Lucy, confused. Did I mistake my name for someone else's? Lucy was smiling at me nodding. It was like I was in a whirlpool in the ocean about to be dragged out to sea and swallowed up.

"Lucy. What is this? I'm meant to be speaking?" The audience was beginning to applaud now and as I looked up at the woman on stage she was standing there smiling at me and clapping. Clapping for me to arrive on stage and speak to these women.

"Lucy. I demand to know what is going on! How can you do this to me?" I was mad and hurt and embarrassed.

"They want you to talk to the audience about you and what you are passionate about. That's all you have to do Soph. You can do that, can't you? Remember... you are already enough. You can do this Sophie."

As if in a fog, I made my way up to the stage and stood in front of the hundreds of women who were eagerly waiting to hear what I had to say. If only they knew, I was waiting for the same thing.

APPLE PIE WITH LUCY

)( )( )( )( )( )(

"Well Grandma Lucy... that was something," I said still stunned by what I just experienced.

"You did so well Sophie! See, it wasn't so hard."

"Not in the end. But, I will NEVER forget that as long as I live." We were walking across the church grounds toward the car park.

"That's exactly right. You won't." Lucy smiled at me.

The penny dropped. "I developed a new story didn't I Lucy?"

"You sure did Soph. You sure did." She was smiling proudly from ear to ear. I wasn't sure if she was smiling because of what I'd done or because of what she managed to pull off with getting me on stage to talk.

The Principle of New Stories

"But how did you know I would create one which would empower me? I mean, I could've refused to get up there and instead felt so humiliated I could have a new story in my storybook that disempowered me for the rest of my life!"

"I knew you would get up there Sophie."

"How did you know?"

"Because I would bet my last dollar that one of your stories is the need to look good. You would have wanted everyone to know you could handle it... even if on the inside you were ready to throw up."

I laughed. I was only okay with all that had transpired because after I finished speaking I actually felt pretty good. I did a good job and the crowd loved what I had to say. Some women even approached me later and told me how much I impacted them. That felt good.

"Well, don't ever think of doing anything like that again," I half threatened, pointing my finger at her before I wrapped my arm around her and kissed her on the cheek.

"So, what's your new story Sophie?"

APPLE PIE WITH LUCY

I took a deep breath. This was all quite an experience. "I'm not quite sure about the story. But, what I learned is that it wasn't so bad. You know... getting up there. Well... that was *really* bad. But, I mean after I was up there and after I started speaking it was great. I really loved it. I guess my story is, I *can*. I *am* good enough. I guess that's my new story... I am good enough."

"That's what I like to hear. You did great today Sophie. I'm very proud of you. We will talk some more about all this tomorrow. Okay?"

"Thanks Lucy. Yes, see you tomorrow. At the meditation room, right?"

"Yep. See you there," she confirmed as she caught up with more women she knew. *She's so sweet.*

Time to head home. I think a bubble bath is in order and a good glass of wine. I feel kinda good about myself. I think I was actually pretty good considering it was my first time in that setting. Wait! I can definitely do it again! For goodness sake... I used to speak at my company conferences all the time!

7

The Principle of Significance

"Who you are is already enough. You are beautifully and
wonderfully made."

I was meeting my grandmother in about an hour and I still hadn't read the readings for the next principle. I have noticed how many things I'm always leaving to the last minute and then it adds stress to my life.

After a quick read I hurried to meet my grandmother and arrived just in time. I hoped Grandma Lucy was planning on explaining today's principle, because I didn't have much of a grasp on it. The concepts seemed so much easier to understand when she explained them anyway. *I did the same thing yesterday! I am really not taking this reading seriously enough.*

"Good morning Sophie."

"Hi Grandma Lucy. You okay?"

"Yes. I'm fine. Just a silly cold. I'll be fine." She was always in such a great mood. She took my coat and motioned for me to follow her. Plans had changed and we were now meeting at her home. She wasn't feeling well today and so she asked we spend our time at her house instead.

"How is my women's inspirational speaker?" She called back over her shoulder as she moved from the front of the house to the kitchen in the back.

"Very funny," I said, making a face. I hung up my coat and followed her.

"I'm being serious. You are. You just spoke yesterday at a women's conference for goodness sake. How much more evidence do you need?" She remarked with a stern seriousness.

I took a seat in my usual place, on one of the breakfast chairs. "I guess so Lucy. I never thought of it like that. I kind of just thought of it as an exercise to prove a point. You know... so I would have an experience to create a new story for myself," I said in defense.

The Principle of Significance

"Well, that was just part of it. You can create whatever story you want. That's the beauty of life. We create all the stories anyway, so we might as well make them be a bunch of stories that empower us. Wouldn't you agree?"

She waited for me to answer. I nodded, smiling.

"Sophie. I know you have heard that life is a journey, not a destination. So, I want you to promise me you won't get caught up with thinking you are going to overnight be a different woman."

"Good advice Grandma Lucy. I promise. It's just that sometimes I wish things *would* be different overnight. I wish sometimes there was a magic pill."

"I used to often wish that. Especially when I was in India in the beginning. I learned though, there is no simple way to success.

"Don't ask for life to be easy Soph. If you're going to ask for anything, ask for the wisdom and strength to get through the tough times. You will be a better person for it. Besides, one thing I know for sure Sophie, it's all about consistency. It's what we do on a daily basis that makes the difference."

Such a wise woman. Why have I not visited with her more often lately? I am kind of glad we are meeting here, because she is always baking. Today was no different. I could smell it as I walked in. It was apple pie again.

"Consistency huh? When can we *consistently* eat that apple pie I know you have baking Lucy?"

She smiled at me. "Very funny! Soon my child. It's about fifteen minutes away from being done. Let's catch up on the last principle from yesterday before we have pie and talk about the next principle, shall we?" She motioned for us to move to the living room.

"Perfect!"

I took a seat in one of the leather sofas while Grandma Lucy added another piece of wood to the fire place, stoking it. Sparks flew and she didn't flinch a bit.

She took a seat opposite me. "So, how was your night after your big day yesterday?"

"It was good. I was pretty exhausted actually. I really wanted to share my experience with John but I just didn't think he would've understood the way it all came about. I think he may have thought you were kind of mean for doing what you did." I said, smiling at her.

"I think you might be right about that. I'm glad you didn't tell him. Maybe after you are complete with it all. You want a glass of water? Sorry I didn't offer." She leaned forward ready to get up if I said yes.

"No. I'm fine. I will wait for the apple pie and might even have a cup of tea with you." She made a surprised face, letting her eyes grow big in her head. She loved having fun with me. I just smiled.

I changed the subject, figuring I would kick off this morning's chat with recapping the last principle. "Yeah. From what I experienced yesterday and my readings from Sharesca, I think I'm correct in saying, the principle of new stories is really about choosing to believe who you are is already enough and then creating new stories in your storybook. And the best way for us to create new stories is by having an experience where it affects us emotionally. Is that right?"

"Yes. That's pretty much it. Why do you think it's important to choose to believe you are already enough first?" Lucy shifted in her chair trying to get more comfortable. She had a knee operation last year and so she often feels some discomfort. Especially when it's cold out she says.

"Well, because everything starts with a thought. At some level I must have thought I was good enough to go on stage yesterday, or I would never have gotten up there. If you took me to a NASA space station and asked me to fly six other people to the moon safely I would have absolutely said no. But, I guess I must have thought I could do what I did yesterday. It was just a matter of which thought was going to win out in the end. Right?"

"Yes. I agree with all of that. And now you have a new story that you can do the same thing again. It's now your truth."

"*However*, it could also happen that I don't have the pressure of that same situation and therefore I may not do it again. I believe it was the pressure of the situation that also pushed me into getting up there. Why is that?"

The Principle of Significance

"Great question. Because if you didn't it would have cost you something. There is always a cost to everything we do, or don't do. The cost of *not* getting up there was obviously higher than you getting out of your chair. Could have been just one thing or a combination of all sorts of things. Maybe the embarrassment of staying in your seat when everyone in the room was expecting you to get up. Or the need to look good like I mentioned yesterday."

"That makes sense." I looked out the window into the street. The trees were still bearing the toll winter had weighed upon them. *If only there were palm trees and a beach across the way.* I missed Florida all of a sudden.

"The best way to develop more and more new stories which empower you is to keep doing things which are outside your comfort zone. It's there you are going to have the most emotional experiences. And you will have the most growth. Make sense?"

I leaned forward taking special interest in what she was saying. "It actually does. Scary thought... but it does make sense. I guess it's about being comfortable with getting uncomfortable." I couldn't imagine living *every* day under that sort of pressure. But I could see how much I would grow if I did.

"Now, remember too, you could have made the experience into a different story all together."

"Yes! I could have made up a story that I was embarrassed and you were cruel. It kinda was by the way." I said teasing my grandmother.

"And I was willing to take that risk. Besides, whatever the story, it's always made up and so you can always change it. Remember that." She patted me on the hand. It was a gesture she always did with people. I liked it. It made me feel safe. She added another thought. "Whenever you have an experience of something Soph your subconscious mind is making up a meaning to that experience. Now you're more aware of your thinking you can notice what stories you're creating for your different experiences. It's in those moments you can create a different meaning. With your conscious mind."

"So, what you are saying is I should have more experiences where I'm outside my comfort zone. Then, when I have an emotional response - and I will because I am outside my comfort zone - I get to participate in the story I am creating in that moment about my emotional experience. I can either make it mean xyz or I can make it mean abc?" I wasn't sure if I got what she was saying.

"Yep, that's what I'm saying. What story we make up subconsciously is based on whether our experience matches what we think it should be like or not. So, being aware of that allows you to notice and then readjust and make up a story which empowers you."

"Okay. So, when I was *forced* to speak in front of all those women," I said trying to be funny. I knew I wasn't being forced. "if I had an experience I *thought* was a horrible one, that in that moment, I could have changed it and made up a different story?"

"Yes. Let me ask you a question. What was the most important thing you learned from reading the notes?" Lucy said changing the subject.

I shifted my focus and thought about her question. "The most powerful thing I got from reading the notes is... hang on... let me read it straight from there. I don't remember it that well." I pulled the book from my handbag and read to my grandmother. "God made us uniquely significant and gave us the ability to create." I added looking up at my grandmother. "What I got from this is we each have a purpose to fulfill with a unique significance to do it. I get to create a life of significance in accordance with my purpose. I just love that notion. I finally get that I have a purpose here. There *is* a reason why I exist. Feels kinda scary... but at the same time I feel... special. " I said trying not to sound too vain.

Lucy smiled at me. "That's great Soph. Sorry to interrupt. I forgot to put the timer on and I think the pie is more than ready. You want some now? I know you like it really hot."

"I sure do!" I said getting up to follow Lucy to the kitchen.

We dished up our pie and returned to the comfort of the sofas we were sitting in.

Careful not to burn my mouth, I took a mouthful of pie and returned my thoughts to the principle of significance. "Obviously tomorrow is when I will learn more about the principle of purpose. But, I'm struggling to separate them. They go hand-in-hand it seems," I said implying a question I would like answered.

"Yes. I agree. They do go hand-in-hand because the purpose you have been assigned also makes you significant, does it not?"

"Yeah. My purpose or *assignment* is unique only to me. That in itself gives me a sense of significance. It makes *me* unique. Therefore makes *me* significant."

"Right. However, would you say, even without looking at the fact you have a special and extremely unique purpose, that you have significance anyway?"

"Well.. what makes me so significant? I mean this isn't one of those times where you're going to tell me 'I'm special and not like any of the other children' are you? I'm not six anymore Lucy."

She chuckled. "Maybe. But, so what if I was? You *are* special." She started into her own apple pie after giving it some time to cool. I wasn't sure who liked Lucy's infamous apple pie more.

She continued without allowing me to disagree. I screwed up my nose smiling at her. "You know Sophie, you *are* one of *those* people. You just haven't stepped into all of who you were made to make manifest in this world."

"One of which people?" I wasn't sure where she was going with her comment.

"The ones to whom you compare yourself."

"What do you mean?" I was confused.

"Remember when we were talking about the principle of self-acceptance? And I said, putting others on a pedestal does nothing to empower you?" she asked rhetorically. "Well, I would like to bring up another point about *unfair comparisons.*"

I motioned for her to continue.

"As you mentioned, we have great significance placed on the inside of every one of us. However, some of us are more accepting of owning our significance than others. That's why I said Oprah deserved to be... I think I used the words respected and admired. No one is *better* than anyone else. She is simply choosing to own her significance and perhaps you are not. However, when we compare where we are now and where someone else is in their journey, that's what I refer to as *unfair comparisons*. For a start, comparing yourself to someone else is just the same as putting someone on a pedestal. It can be extremely disempowering and leaves you feeling inadequate. But, even worse, comparing where you are and where Oprah is in her professional journey is like comparing apples and bananas. They might be both fruit, but that's about the only ounce of similarity as you're going to get." She paused. It looked like she was searching her mind to see if there was anything else she wanted to add. All her searching paid off. "And that is some of the reason why you are stuck."

Neither of us spoke for a while. I looked out into the front yard of my grandmother's home.

Grandma Lucy snapped me from my thoughts with another one of her great bumper sticker phrases. This one was actually pretty good. "I like to think disappointment is the gap which exists between expectations and reality."

"Well, I am no psychologist... but it seems to be a natural human behavior. It seems that when we are not owning our greatness, significance, and uniqueness, we often compare ourselves to other people."

"Sure. And maybe it's our way of not having to really do something with our own brilliance," Lucy remarked.

"Ouch! That's pretty harsh Lucy." I stopped for a moment and gave thought to how this applied to me. "When *I* don't own my greatness then *I* compare myself to someone who is where *I* want to be so then *I* can stay stuck." *Ugh! I am not sure I like being so aware of my thoughts and how and why I do things.*

Lucy smiled at me. "I agree. That's why you are feeling so empty Soph. That and you are not fulfilling your God-given purpose."

"Why do you always say *God-given* purpose? Why not just *purpose*?" I asked as I placed my empty plate on the coffee table.

"I believe when I'm specific I am referring to a purpose which does good in the world. I believe those men who flew those planes into the World Trade Center, years back, believed they were living on purpose. But, it was extremely destructive. I don't believe it was a God-given purpose. But, hey, that's just me. You know my faith Soph. I am all about God and his love for us. Even if it doesn't always seem like that through our own eyes sometimes.

"Let me get back to what you were talking about earlier around significance. From memory there was a question for you to journal on last night. Something like, 'is the underlying theme of your storybook one of significance?'. How did you go with answering that question?"

"Great question Grandma Lucy. I realized I really don't think I am *that* significant. My storybook seems to be filled with lots of stories about how I am not enough, who am I to be doing *that*, why am I any more special than the next person, yada yada yada."

"Sophie, even though something may have happened to you where someone hurt you or there are things you have done that you are not proud of, it doesn't take anything away from your significance. You are significant no matter what. Significance, or greatness, is not some elusive thing only a few select people possess. It exists in all of us and it's up to us to choose to own it."

I just couldn't get my head around this. "But, aren't we measured by what things we have done and what we have given back to society?"

"You are putting the cart before the horse again Soph. Just like we talked about a couple of days back." She waited for me to recall our previous meetings before continuing. "Remember we talked about how first it's necessary to *believe* you are smart enough before you will ever apply for a certain job. I know I didn't use this as an example, but our storybook about ourselves is such a part of who we think we are, we will even use it to chose our husbands. If a woman believes she is a number two in grading herself on a scale between one, being the lowest, and ten, being the highest, do you think she is going to be on the look out for a number ten when she's looking to date a man?"

I smiled at the picture I had in my head of a woman who lives in a trailer asking out a man who is a billionaire living on the ocean in Malibu. They wouldn't even socialize in the same places. "No. I can't see that happening. Unless she was digging for gold."

"Even then she has to believe she deserves having all that money and to live that lifestyle."

"Good point."

"Let me relate this to significance. Do you remember the explanation Sharesca used in the book about significance?"

"Yeah. She said when we believe we're significant we believe are we enough, we're worthy and unique. But it's more about a divine appointment for us to be here on earth possessing the strengths and the uniqueness of each of us. It's kinda hard to explain.

"Oh! and she said when we truly get we are significant we will think, feel and act as if." I added.

"As if what?" Lucy asked.

"You know... we show up in our everyday life just being significant. We don't have to pretend anymore. We don't have to *wish* we were. And we certainly don't have to worry someone is *more* than we are. Everyone is significant in their own way." I was surprised I had remembered what the notes said.

Lucy smiled and nodded in agreement before she added her own thoughts. "When we choose to own who we are is significant, then it has nothing to do with what we are *doing* or what we have done. However, once we own our significance we will then naturally extend ourselves in our feelings and actions and live a life which is significant. One which is congruent with our God-given purpose."

"That seems to make sense."

We both sat in silence for a while. I think Lucy was letting me chew on what we just discussed.

I broke the silence. "I guess owning my significance allows my presence to shine. The way I figure it... I am better off being me, everyone else has already been taken, right?!" I looked at my grandmother who was beaming at me. She was so proud. I could tell.

"You will do great things in this world Soph. Great things."

The Principle of Significance

"Thanks Lucy. There were two aspects to significance I read about in Sharesca's notes," I said looking to take the attention away from myself.

"Correct. Do you have some questions about that or would you like me to explain it through?"

"If you could talk it out for me that would be great Lucy."

"One thing I know for sure is *all* people, no matter where they live in the world or how they live, want the same thing. They want to feel significant as a unique and special individual and also to *live* a life of significance." She had spent time with a lot of people from all around the world in her days traveling with my grandfather. "What do *you* think it means to live a life of significance?" she asked.

"I think it means to do something important. Something that makes a difference in the world. If I lived a significant life it would mean my life meant something while I was here."

"That is simply it. There is really nothing more to it. And I really want you to carry that thought with you as you go into the next principle. When I was a young woman I was all caught up on figuring out what my purpose was. God-given or not. I just wanted to know why I was here. That became a lot of pressure. I mean, imagine living your whole life doing something that was not what you were meant to be doing? I didn't want to have that regret when I got to the end of my life.

"After a few years of trying to figure out what my purpose was, your grandfather said something very wise that I will never forget. He said 'Lucy, just live your best life by always looking to make the world better than when you got here. Then, as you do that, your purpose will reveal itself. Don't try and figure it out with that noggin of yours. You are going to make yourself crazy.'"

"That's some great advice Lucy. He was a great man. You know, I came into all of this not knowing I really did want to figure out why I am here. I thought I could just figure out why I'm so unhappy a lot of the time. But, this is a huge part of it. So, going into the next principle looking at it with that perspective will definitely help me."

The Principle of Significance

)()()()()()(

I was meeting John for dinner tonight. We hadn't gone out for dinner, just the two of us, for a very long time. We arranged for Lily to sleep at my parent's place so we could have the whole night to ourselves.

We were meeting at six and so I still had a few hours to implement the last principle. Being that it was about significance, I decided I would do something I felt was significant for someone else. I chose to go down to the homeless shelter in downtown Milwaukee. It shows how disconnected I am from my own community - I had to 'google' where the closest one was located.

It was a daunting experience and definitely outside my comfort zone. It's funny how often when we give, whether it be our time or our resources, it ends up being more rewarding for us than it is for the recipient. At least that's how it felt for me.

APPLE PIE WITH LUCY

8

The Principle of Purpose

"All that is necessary for the triumph of evil is that good men do nothing" Edmund Burke

"In order to be truly happy we must stand for something bigger than ourselves."

It was John's alarm that woke me this morning. I rolled over to see why he hadn't switched it off. He wasn't in the bed. Then I remembered.

John and I went to dinner last night as planned and for some reason whenever we spend any one-on-one time like that, we always end up arguing. He decided he would sleep in one of the kid's rooms when we got home.

The argument started because I shared with him my meetings with Grandma Lucy, what she was teaching me

131

and the magical place her and I had been meeting at. I also told him about my homeless shelter experience. He was upset about something I said and when I told him the story of speaking at the church and how my grandmother 'surprised' me the way she did - he lost it. He started telling me my grandmother was half crazy and how that was a horrible thing to do and I shouldn't be spending any more time with her.

Maybe he left for work already. Good! I don't want to see him this morning. I hope he has left for work. I can't believe he needs to make everything I do seem so stupid.

Curiosity got the better of me, so I got up and quietly went in search. I prepared myself for what I would say in case I did see him. I would need to make sure he knew I was still mad at him. I looked in all the kid's rooms first which were located at the far end of the house, past the kitchen. No sign of him there. I checked to see if his phone and wallet were still on the counter where he always left them. No keys, no wallet.

Part of me was disappointed he wasn't still at the house. I'm not sure if it was to have another chance at having the last word, or because I actually missed him and I was sorry for my harsh words spoken in the crossfire.

I decided I would make myself some breakfast and read all about the principle for today. This would be the first time I had read it well in advance of meeting my grandmother. It was a nice distraction from how I felt toward John. Although, part of me felt like quitting and not finishing this with Lucy.

I opened the notes. It read:

The Principle of Purpose
Day 5

You were birthed into this world at this very time in history for a reason. There are no coincidences about your existence. You are here to solve a problem and leave behind a legacy which continues to impact the world. To significantly leave it better than how you found it when you got here.

I stopped reading and thought about the powerful words that were leaping of the page and dancing around my head.

There were only a couple of days left and I started to feel really connected to myself. It had been a long time since I felt this way. I felt connected not only to myself, but somehow I felt connected to my *better* self. That was of course before John made me feel like what I was doing was stupid.

I read the rest of the notes before I drove to meet my grandmother.

)()()()()()(

The Principle of Purpose

"Sophie?"

"Oh! Hi there Lucy." I called out to my grandmother who had just pulled into the parking lot and started out of her car.

"You beat me here. That's a first." She said smiling at me.

I helped her out of her car, took her handbag and closed the car door, locking it with her keys. "There's a first time for everything, they say," I said flatly as I kissed her on the cheek.

Grandma Lucy took my hand as we started walking toward the meditation room. "I like it Sophie," she said, stroking my hand. "I really do." She slowed and looked at me smiling. Almost with a I-feel-sorry-for-you smile and added, "That is one thing you have always been challenged by since as long as I can remember."

"Being late?" I asked as we came to a stop. I looked down at my feet and started to kick at the dead grass with my shoe. "Yeah, I know. Everyone knows. And things are

135

going to be different now. A lot of things are going to be different," I said, looking up at her with a renewed sense of hope for my seemingly problematic life. "They already are." I added, trying to muster the enthusiasm I had been experiencing for my life earlier this week.

"Great to hear Sophie." We started off again, linking arms.

"You feeling better today Lucy?" I asked as we drew closer to the meditation room.

"Yes. Much better. Thank you. It was nice to have pie with you again yesterday. And on Monday I have another surprise for you."

I stopped walking and stood still looking at her before I protested. "Lucy. It isn't going to be something to do with getting *uncomfortable* is it? I don't know if I can do something like that twice in the same week."

She just laughed.

I didn't see the humor in it. "Seriously. Please tell me it's going to be a nice surprise. Like a pedicure or something."

The Principle of Purpose

"It's not a pedicure Sophie. Don't worry. Come on. Let's get you into the warmth. It's supposed to snow tonight. Did you hear about that?" She said, changing the subject.

"Yes. And I'm not happy about it." *I hate living here. Why do I even bother?*

We linked arms and walked to the meditation room, entered and got comfortable.

"What's going on this morning Soph? It really is true, your eyes are the windows to your soul. Plus, the sad puppy dog look you have on your face is a giveaway too."

That made me smile and for a moment I shifted out of the shadow of the joyless feeling I had wrapped myself in.

"John and I had a huge argument last night. He is mad I am doing this with you and thinks it's stupid. He just made me so mad. I really don't know if I feel like doing this with you Lucy."

Lucy didn't say anything. She just listened, taking in what I was saying.

"He makes me feel so worthless sometimes. He never supports me in what I'm doing. I think he would rather I just get a job, because that is safe in his mind. He doesn't trust me to take any risks." I fell silent and looked up at the painting on the wall in front of me. It was the same one I had been looking at each time we were here.

We both sat in silence for a while before I asked Lucy a question. "So, what do you think I should do Lucy?"

"About what?"

"Don't you think he is being a real pain in the ass right now?"

"Let me ask you a question," she said, not answering my question. "Do you feel empowered right now Sophie?"

I was quick to answer. "No way! John never empowers me."

"That's not what I asked Soph. I simply asked if you felt empowered right now?"

"No. I don't"

The Principle of Purpose

"Only we get to choose the way we react or respond to something someone says or does. John doesn't *make* you think or feel anything Soph. You are responsible for all of that. When you allow someone else to affect the way you are feeling then you give away your power. Don't give away your power so quickly. That's what causes disempowerment. The moment you feel like giving up on something, you must dig deep to change your thinking and how you feel. Every time you quit it just adds more evidence to your stories that don't support your greatness."

"Yeah... but you should have heard him. He was saying you're half crazy and I'm wasting my time." Surely she would be on my side now. I just threw him under the bus. Besides, this isn't about me wanting to quit. This is about John making me feel like what I want to do isn't important.

"It's irrelevant what he said Soph. Why is it that what someone thinks of you matters so much?"

I wasn't sure if she was asking a rhetorical question or not. I decided I wouldn't answer. Besides, I don't care what other people think of me.

APPLE PIE WITH LUCY

Lucy didn't say anything for a while. We both just sat there.

I guess I do care what John thinks. I want him to support me with what I'm doing. Maybe he thinks this is just another thing I am doing to be distracted. I think he thinks I could've just gotten a job by now and started earning additional income, which would definitely help right now.

"You're right Lucy. I reacted very quickly to what he was saying last night. Heck... I probably even threw the first insult. I get offended quite quickly." I felt bad all of a sudden for poor John. *Just when I felt great about my future, our future, I went and reacted like that. Ugh!*

"Don't beat yourself up Soph. Every time someone doesn't agree with what you are doing or what you think, you are just going to get all mad? And then get all sad about how you got all mad? That's not going to empower you in life, Soph. Don't make most of what happens in life a reflection of who you are as a woman. John is entitled to his opinion. When you stand in your own power you can

140

then respond in a grounded and responsible manner. That is *not* what you did last night... by the sound of it."

"You are spot on Lucy. Thank you. I didn't respond in a responsible manner. I guess that's something I can reflect on. *How* I handled everything." I wished I could do last night all over again. "I'm not going to quit by the way." I added.

"Well, we learn best by experiencing something... as you know. Shall we move on with the next principle?"

I nodded.

"Did you read about the next principle Sophie? The principle of purpose? That's where we are up to, isn't it?" she asked as she propped herself up on a couple of pillows. She was almost laying down on her side.

"Yes it is. And I sure did. I was very productive this morning Lucy. Lily stayed at Mom's last night and so I had some time this morning to do as I pleased." I remarked.

I had a sudden sense of urgency. There were some things I wanted to get done today. I was going to do some research on where I could volunteer my speaking. Plus, I needed to have a chat with John and apologize.

"Great! Let's do it," she said sitting up and clasping her hands together eagerly.

I got started with where I thought she might like to start. "I read all about the principle of purpose and I tell you, I'm glad you told me what you did yesterday. About the advice grand papa gave you. That really helped me with this principle."

"Good good," she said almost staring at me. She looked like she was pondering something else. She turned and looked into the fireplace and then said slowly, "There are problems in the world that are in drastic need of solutions Soph." Her tone was serious. Almost as if she was saddened by what she was thinking. She looked back at me and continued. "And if each of us were to be connected with our God-given purpose, these problems would cease to exist," she said almost pleading with me to see the solution she saw.

I looked at the painting hanging on the wall. *I just don't know if I agree. She sure does believe we are all here to solve a problem.*

The Principle of Purpose

She smiled at me and spoke with less heaviness. "But, I think it helps if we go out into the world with the want to help in a significant way. And then the purpose we are here for will reveal itself. Like I said yesterday."

"I have never really thought about it as much as I have this week. I want the world to be better because I was here. I want my work, my life, my family to mean something."

Lucy nodded. "You and your light are not meant to be hidden. Would you ever place a lamp *under* your bedside table? Of course not. Then why would you ever hide your light from the world. And, don't be waiting for all the traffic lights to be green before you start living that way either. The best thing is to just start." She patted me on the knee.

"I'm not really sure *where* to start. I'm going to do some research this afternoon about where I can start speaking, but I don't even know what I want to inspire women about." I still felt confused about what I wanted.

"It will all unfold. Have you ever seen the movie with that handsome actor... what's his name?"

I just waited for her to think of it. She really didn't give me much to go on.

"Harrison Ford. That's it! He was in those movies called Indiana Jones. Have you seen them?"

"Uh huh." I remember seeing them as a kid. I have three brothers and so we watched them over and over.

"Do you remember the scene where he had to take a step and trust the next step would appear?" she asked enthusiastically.

"Yeah. I sure do. That was a great scene. I think he is looking for the cup of life from memory." I loved movies. Going to the movies with John was a common 'date night' occurrence. Not very exciting I know. But, after a while we both just got casual I guess. Or boring.

"That's what will happen when you step out toward your passion and your talent with a true desire to want to make a difference in the world. I really believe that. I have seen evidence of it in my own life." She was sitting up now. Grandma Lucy really did have a passion for seeing people live their best life.

The Principle of Purpose

"Wow. I can't imagine taking risks in my own life. Like he did anyways. That seems pretty scary Lucy."

"Anything worth your soul's fulfillment is worth taking a risk on. Big risks. The bigger the better." She sat back beaming. She was sure of what she believed and she did have some great evidence of a fulfilled life.

We both sat in silence for a moment. I was musing about what Grandma Lucy just said. *I wonder what Lucy thinks about this whole fixing a problem theory.*

I broke the silence. "Going back to what you said before about how there are problems in the world that need solutions. Do you *really* agree with what Sharesca believes? That we are all here to solve a problem?" I still wasn't completely sold on the whole we-are-here-for-a-specific-purpose thing.

She leaned forward slightly, taking the question seriously. She pursed her lips thinking about the question, or the answer. I wasn't sure which. She answered slowly. "I do. I really do. And I think the closer we can live authentically to who we are, we have a better chance of knowing ourselves and what our place is in the world.

Besides... more often than not, the answer is right in front of us. There is a reason why some people love to save the whales and others, the trees. And there is a reason why you want to inspire women. It doesn't get much more obvious than that. Why do we spend our lives fighting what is blazingly obvious?!"

"You make a good point Lucy. I mean, maybe *that* is my purpose. Why do I need to think it's any different than that? Maybe I am expecting a big 'ah ha' moment." I sat there thinking. *Maybe I have always known my purpose. I was just complicating it.*

Lucy just sat with me in silence while I was digesting it all. "Well... I'm very happy with letting it all unfold. I don't think I want to get all caught up in trying to figure out what it is. I'm happy for it to reveal itself. And I am equally happy to think maybe, just maybe, I already have it figured out." I was certainly okay with letting go of looking for a dramatic moment in my life where my purpose gets painted in the sky for me. *In fact, I think I have. It doesn't need to be complicated. I am here to inspire women. That's my purpose!*

The Principle of Purpose

Lucy brought me back from my thoughts. "Good for you Soph."

"I think I have figured it out! I think you're right. There is nothing more to it. I'm here to inspire women. End of story." I felt relieved. I was a little anxious too. Now I 'd figured it out I felt as if I have to actually live on purpose.

"I think you taught me something Soph. Maybe you're right. Maybe it's as simple as it needs to be. And I bet you will find you can do that wherever you go. You can inspire women at the grocery store. In fact.. you just inspired me!" she said smiling.

"Lucy? Can I ask you a question?"

"You just did," she said smirking.

"Very funny. I've been thinking about how I go about implementing this principle into my life for today. I'm not sure how to do that. Any chance you could give me a hint?"

She looked at me and put her hand on my shoulder. "Soph. I think you did just implement it."

I was confused. Then it dawned on me. "I did, didn't I Lucy?"

APPLE PIE WITH LUCY

9

The Principle of Dreams

"Dreams are illustrations... from the book your soul is writing about you. " Marsha Norman.

"You see things and say, 'Why?' But I dream things that never were, and I say, 'Why not?'" George Bernard Shaw.

As the week draws near completion I find myself reflecting back on *how* I have undergone this quest and *how* I do life in general. The biggest thing I noticed was how easy it was for me to consider quitting yesterday. I think what happens is I start a lot of things and then quickly get bored and don't complete most things. John always joked, if I didn't have a choice about carrying each of the kids for nine months I might've quit on that too - I complained a *lot* when I was pregnant. Not that I ever thought it was a funny joke, I did think there was some merit to it. It's almost as if when things get too hard, or I lose interest, I don't push through and get it done. I just simply quit. That was a huge wake up call for me.

On an empowering note, I swallowed my pride and apologized to John yesterday for the argument we'd had on our date night. We talked about how things were in our marriage and it was great to finally be open about things we had both swept under the carpet. I did a lot of listening and although I didn't like hearing everything I heard, all in all it was very refreshing. It had been a long time since we talked this way.

Eager to get an early start this morning, I read all about the 'principle of dreams' and arranged for my grandmother to meet me inside the meditation room instead of the parking lot. I was planning on spending some time meditating - not that it would be for long. I have an attention span of a gnat.

The Principle of Dreams

The plan was then to apply the principle immediately, instead of waiting until after Lucy and I had spoken about it. I loved this topic, and I was good at it. I've had many dreams in my life - most of which never grew wings and never got off the ground. Nonetheless, I am a good dreamer. Besides, things felt different for me at the moment and I was willing to keep the momentum rolling. Time to start dreaming with some real clarity and maybe even an action plan.

I opened my journal and put pen to paper. I started thinking about all the things I always wanted to do to inspire women. Over the years I have continued to come back to the same dream. Sharesca talked about that in her notes. She believed that because our dreams come from our soul they are always with us and our thoughts will always return to them until they are fulfilled.

There is no coincidence I was a corporate trainer before I had the kids. I was doing something close to what I had always wanted to do. It's obvious now though I was settling in my life by having that role and not doing what I knew deep down I really wanted to do. Now is my opportunity to change that.

I heard a knock on the old wooden door which kept the treasures of this sacred room from the outside elements. It was Lucy. She had managed to trudge through the snow which fell last night in what I was hoping would be mother natures last ditch attempt at cooling the northern hemisphere. It was almost April after all. Surely spring would grace us with its presence soon.

"Grandma Lucy I should have come and met you. Were the paths cleared? They weren't when I got here. I had become side tracked and lost track of the time. Are you okay?"

"Why are you fussing? Of course I'm fine. Just because I'm about forty years older than you doesn't mean I can't walk in snow."

I wasn't sure if what she just said was sarcasm or not. "Well, I would liked to have helped you. I'm sorry. Glad to see you are here. I'm very excited about today and the principle of dreams."

The Principle of Dreams

"Good! Me too." Grandma Lucy said as she hung up her coat and took a seat by the fire place. It wasn't a wood fed fireplace like Lucy had at her house. It was a gas heater that *looked* like a wood fireplace. Nonetheless, it kept the room wonderfully warm.

I took a seat next to her.

"Did you enjoy the solitude of this place this morning Soph? It's nice isn't it?" She said looking around the room as if she had never seen it before.

"It was lovely. I did some journaling on my dreams. It was great to spend the time with just me," I said beaming.

"Great! So you got some dreams down on paper then?"

"Um... yes," I said as I pulled my journal close to me. I didn't like sharing them with anyone. Not yet anyway.

Lucy looked at me and spoke seriously. "Protect your dreams at all costs Sophie. Don't let anyone tell you can't do them. Sometimes, if someone feels like they themselves can't fulfill their dreams they will look to tear you and yours down."

I nodded, promising I would protect my dreams. "I don't think I have ever experienced that because I have actioned so very few of my dreams. And the ones I have actioned, I tend to quit before anyone else has a chance to deprive me of having it. I seem to have lots of ideas but I never seem to get crystal clear on them. And then I guess I can't very well take action because I'm not really very clear on what it is I want."

"Getting clear on your dream is the first step. It's the excitement of the clarity of your dream which will keep you steadfast during the times when you are challenged. And you will be."

"Why is it then that I've had so much trouble in really clarifying what I want?" I asked hoping for some resolution.

"When we are not okay with who we are Soph then we're not okay with our dreams. Anything that comes from within us, for example a dream, will not be good enough if we don't think we are good enough."

The Principle of Dreams

"That certainly makes sense." I wasn't sure it answered my problem though. "But, the thing is, I do come up with some great dreams. In fact, I am really quite good at the dreaming part. But, that's all that remains... just a dream. When I say there is no clarity, I guess I mean the dream just stays kinda... daydream like. There seems to be no substance to it." I looked to see if she was following me. I wasn't even sure I was following me.

"Are you saying, if you were to start actioning the dream you probably wouldn't know where to start because you aren't even sure the dream has any substance?"

"Yeah. I guess so. I guess I haven't taken most of my dreams serious enough to action. I guess because I have't taken myself serious. I haven't seriously considered I could actually do it."

I had answered my own uncertainty of this conundrum. It made total sense. My dreams didn't have any substance to them because I didn't think I had the ability to fulfill them.

I sat back and looked up at the picture on the wall. *Here I am again. I feel like I am back at square one.*

"Sophie, when we resist who we think we need to be or even who we think we are, then we will resist anything that comes from within us... including our dreams. Go back to what we talked about in the beginning of the week. Be okay with who you are now and trust as you take a step forward you will find the qualities within you to master the dream. If you dreamed the dream Sophie, you have what it takes. It's an extension of who you are authentically. So it makes sense you *do* have what is required to fulfill it. That's why you can't achieve a dream which belongs to someone else. Be sure it's your dream. That it's an extension of you and not something you saw someone else doing and thought 'I would love to do that.'"

"Yeah... I think if I take the focus off myself and focus on what it is my dream can do for others then that will help."

"Great advice Sophie."

I pulled out my book from my handbag. "I loved what Sharesca wrote in her notes." I opened up to the page and read. "A dream is an inspiring picture of the future that energizes your mind, will, and emotions, empowering you

156

to do everything you can to achieve your purpose." I closed the book and smiled at my grandmother.

"It's all perfect. Isn't it?! Did you happen to answer the *Four D's of dreaming* in the exercise for today?"

"Not yet. What are they again?" I was planning on looking into this some more later. Sharesca had identified four aspects to dreaming which she referred to as the 'Four D's of Dreaming'.

"The first is Dominion. Is it your dream, or is it someone else's? Like I just mentioned. The next is Definition. Have you clearly defined it? And then, Dedication. Are you dedicated to see it through to completion? And the last is Direction. Does your dream take you in the direction of your purpose?"

"I have not looked at any of that yet. I had planned to check back in with my dream after we met. I did some journaling this morning before you got here. I think I will go back and check in to be sure it meets all those four aspects."

"You okay? You seem flat."

"No. I'm good. Just feeling a little uneasy about it all. I don't want to go back to the way things were before we met this week Lucy. Or to have another 'episode' like I did the other day."

"You are doing great. Cut yourself some slack. Stop taking everything so serious."

I smiled. *I do tend to take things seriously.*

"I don't have to be anywhere until lunch. Would you like to look at those four aspects of a dream with me now?" she asked. But it was not really a question. It was more like a statement. I think she wanted to talk about it more than I did.

"That would be good grandma Lucy. I'd like that." I got out my notebook to take some notes.

"As I just mentioned, there are four parts to a dream Sharesca believed are important. Let's start with the first one, dominion. Ask yourself, do you dominate your dream? Is it yours?" I got ready to take notes. "How about I just go through it all and then you can go ahead and answer these questions in your journaling later?"

158

The Principle of Dreams

I stopped and looked up at her. "That's fine. I don't think I have any questions about any of it. I think it's just a matter of answering it all for myself." I put my journal to my side and focused my attention on Lucy.

"I agree. Getting back to the first one. Is it *your* dream? Do you dominate it? Is it a part of who you are? Be sure you are not trying to live out someone else's dream. That'll never work." She was shaking her head as if she was recalling her own detriment. "What else is there?" She pursed her lips and looked at the fire place. "Oh yeah! Be sure it's crystal clear. Oh! wait... that's the second one. Definition. Be sure you clearly define it. And I mean use as many descriptive words as possible. So every time you go back and read it you are filled with enthusiasm. Be as creative as possible and describe every part of the dream. Plus, you want to be specific because then you'll have less chance of being distracted and thinking up another dream.

"The third thing is dedication. You will need to be dedicated to it. But, what Sharesca meant by dedicated is, even in this early stage be sure you are *prepared* to be dedicated to it. I guess that's why it's important to know that it's *your* dream before you start making it happen."

I was listening to her intently with my pen in my mouth. "Good point. I can see how important it is to be sure it's my dream." I often see what others are doing and think it would be a great idea for me.

"Yes. And trusting yourself and your own ideas is invaluable Soph. That's why I said when we are okay with who we are then we will be okay with the dreams we have within us," she reminded me.

"The last one, direction, is pretty obvious. Is your dream taking you in the direction of your purpose?"

I was confused. "But, how do I know if my dream is taking me in the direction of my purpose if I don't know what my purpose is? *If* I didn't know what my purpose was."

"Great question Soph. Think of it like this. Remember we talked about going about your life looking to live a life which is significant?"

I nodded. "Uh huh."

The Principle of Dreams

"Well, look to do that, then carve out your dream. Don't be too concerned with trying to figure out what is the 'right' thing to do. Doing something is better than doing nothing. At least you will be moving. No good if you are in park all the time," she said as she took a tissue from her pocket and blew her nose. She was still battling the remnants of her cold.

"What do you mean by significant again?" This part of the quest was still bugging me. I think I was still getting caught up on knowing my purpose. *My purpose is to inspire. Sophie - you already know what it is. Don't try and figure it out anymore than you already have.*

"I believe it means to live your life to your full potential. Getting yourself out of the way and constantly being outside your comfort zone, as you make a difference in the lives of others. We are measured not by what we get Soph, but instead by what we give."

I sat there and pondered what my grandmother said. *I really have been so very selfish about my life. I have been so worried about how unhappy I am. Yet I have so much. There are women out there who have nothing.*

Lucy could see I was troubled. "What's going on Soph? You want to talk about something?"

I hesitated and then spoke slowly. "I have been so selfish Lucy. I even visited a homeless shelter for women the other day and still I can only think of myself. It's time to put others first Grandma Lucy."

"Don't be so hard on yourself Sophie. You are a loving wife and mother. You've been so very giving to your family and have done an extraordinary job of raising them. You even moved here for John's career. I wouldn't say you are selfish.

"Authentically you are very generous Soph. And you have a beautiful spirit." She added. "In fact, you have most likely been putting your dreams on hold for everyone else!"

I smiled at her and welcomed the idea my grandmother had suggested. *I HAVE been putting my family first. Which is fine. But, now I can start to focus on what I want. That's not selfish.*

Lucy snapped me from my thoughts. "Sophie. I will have to get going now." She got up and grabbed her jacket and gloves. "I'll see you tomorrow." She said almost as a question.

"Yes... see you tomorrow." I got up and helped her into her jacket, kissed her on the cheek and gave her a long and loving hug. She smelled like vanilla. "I love you Grandma Lucy," I added as she headed out the door.

"I love you too Soph."

APPLE PIE WITH LUCY

10

The Principle of Now

"There is power in choosing constant forward motion while embracing the moment."

I was meeting Grandma Lucy again this morning as I had done every day for the last six days. Today was the last day of the quest and to say I was apprehensive would be an understatement. There were a mix of emotions I was feeling and most of them I couldn't quite articulate.

We were planning on meeting at her house and then we would both drive together to where she said the surprise was waiting for me. She wanted me to first share with her my dream and which of the top twenty action steps I was going to implement first.

APPLE PIE WITH LUCY

The final principle was all about the power of getting started. It was called the 'principle of now'. I read all about it last night and did my final journaling which included jotting down the list of actionable steps I believed I would need to take in order to action my dream. It was a relatively new experience for me.

I arrived at Lucy's house and rang the door bell. I could hear music coming from inside and knew I would have to turn it down when I got in. My grandmother was a little hard of hearing and she loved playing her music loud. The door flew open and Lucy appeared. She was dressed in a beautiful pant suit.

"Wow Lucy. You look amazing!"

"So do you Sophie. Come on in."

"I can't believe today is the last day of my quest Lucy."

"It has been quite a week though, hasn't it?" Grandma Lucy gestured for me to take a seat on the couch. She turned off her music and sat next to me.

"Sure has Lucy." I said reflecting back on all the ups and downs of the week.

The Principle of Now

"I am so very excited to hear about what you wrote for your big dream Sophie. You want to go ahead and read it to me?"

I hesitated a little. I really did want to read it to her as I was excited about what I journaled. I was just a little embarrassed. Maybe she would think it was foolish.

"Let me get us some hot tea and then you can share with me. Okay?"

"Um... yeah. Sure. Do you want a hand with that?"

"Nope. I got it." She headed off to the kitchen to make us both some hot tea. She loved drinking tea. Anyone would think she were English.

I waited for her in the living room. The room, not unlike the rest of her house, was beautifully kept. She always took care of not only her appearance, but also the appearance of her home.

I started to read over the dream I journaled on. While it created some excitement in my body, the thought of achieving all of it made me sick to my stomach. However, the action steps I came up with sure made the mission seem much more achievable.

APPLE PIE WITH LUCY

Lucy returned with the hot tea and some shortbread cookies. No apple pie today.

"This weather is supposed to shift next week. Should see some of this snow melt in no time." Lucy took a sip of her hot tea.

"I'm glad to hear that. Would you like to hear about what I wrote Grandma Lucy? I just read it over and I'm kind of excited about it actually."

"Yes. I sure do. Go ahead."

So I did just that. I read her my dream for my future including all of my hopes for inspiring women all around the world, writing books, appearing on television shows like Oprah - which was the scariest thing to add to my dream. I even had mention of how I envisioned myself speaking in front of thousands of women in stadiums.

I finished reading and rested my journal on my lap. "Why are you crying Grandma Lucy?" I got her a tissue from my handbag.

"They are tears of joy Sophie. I am so proud of you and I can see you doing all of those things." She smiled and took my hand in hers.

"Thanks Lucy. I feel like you really do believe I can do all this. If I don't think about it... I think I can too."

Lucy started laughing. "Well, that would be the best thing to do I guess. Just don't think about it."

"That's a good point," I said, adding myself to the laughter.

"But, it's going to take some real work on your part Sophie. Nothing happens by shear accident. There are never any overnight success stories. There are no shortcuts to accomplishing our dreams."

"Yeah... I think that's one thing I have realized this week Lucy."

"What's that exactly?"

"I think in the past I was looking for a lotto ticket solution to achieving my dreams. Wishing constantly for the *one thing* which would make me successful overnight. I realized a couple of other things too. The first is, I am just as deserving and talented to be successful as some of the people I admire. And secondly, I don't have to wait until I have everything all figured out. In fact, I need to get started right where I am and to keep my mission or my dream clearly in front of me."

"Yes. First, you must decide on what it is you want. And having a healthy acceptance and confident ownership of who you are, you can go about fulfilling your dream."

"Sure." My mind started to wander elsewhere.

"What is on your mind Sophie?"

"Huh?" Lucy snapped me from my thoughts and back to the present. "Well... I didn't have too much trouble with the dreaming part. Which has never really been much of an issue for me. And I know I have said this before, but the biggest issue is I don't put these dreams into action."

Lucy nodded. "I understand. Let me ask you a question. Do you have a healthier belief you can achieve them now, after spending this week together?"

"I sure do. But I think I have a long way to go."

"Ok, and like I said during the week... don't think that overnight you will just wake up and be a different woman. You are on the right track though Sophie. Remember, it's all about consistency. It's about consistently being outside your comfort zone and creating new emotional experiences for yourself so you can create new stories. That's the key."

"Yeah. You're right." *I sure am glad I have this book from Sharesca I can refer to.* "I'm glad I have you in my life Lucy. You are a real gift."

"Thanks Sophie."

"I did have some trouble though with my action steps. I was fine with writing down a bunch of things I know could get me moving toward my dream. But if I really stopped and thought about implementing them I felt myself become a little overwhelmed." I paused, collecting my thoughts.

"Let me give you an example. I said in my dream I want to inspire women all over the world. But, I don't even know what I am going to talk about. I don't have a clue what my message is!"

"Good point. I am glad you noticed that Soph."

"You mean you noticed it too? That I wasn't being very specific?"

"Uh huh. Sure did. Here's the thing Sophie. There is a freeing power in making a choice. Even if you are not sure it's the *right* one, just choose something that inspires *you* and make *that* your message. Don't over think it. Remember, when you are confused about something it means you are resisting it. So, when you are not clear about something, check in and ask yourself what it is you are resisting. It's a great habit to establish to monitor how you are living life."

"Okay. I have a question about that statement. How I'm doing something is a reflection of what I'm thinking, isn't it?"

Lucy smiled at me. "Yes. But, why do you think that?"

"Because *how* I am doing something is an action. Which results from a thought. For example, I noticed the other day I was procrastinating about doing something. So, I looked at what thoughts I had other than 'I can't be bothered doing this.'"

"And what did you discover?"

"I didn't. I got stuck there. But I thought I did a pretty good job noticing it was probably from a thought or a story I made up about myself!" I said in my defense.

Lucy laughed. "True."

I waited for her to tell me what my story was but she didn't volunteer the information.

"So, what is it Lucy? What thought did I have? Other than the one where I thought I couldn't be bothered doing something."

She shrugged her shoulders. "I don't know Soph. Only you know those answers. I would just be guessing." She smiled at me with one of those it's-okay-you'll-figure-it-out smiles.

I smiled too and had another question for her. "You think I'm just better off starting with whatever ideas I have right now? You know... in regards to my dream."

"Yes that's what I would do. Be proactive in life rather than feeling like you are at effect to all the things that are happening. That way your message will reveal itself anyway. It will become more absolute as you evolve into your dream. It's important Soph that you dedicate yourself to your dream every single day."

"That's what it said in Sharesca's notes. To be honest, I was still hoping maybe you would have a magic wand for me today. Given it's the last day and all." I smiled at her and took a sip of my tea. It wasn't hot anymore and didn't taste too good.

"And what would you like that magic wand to be able to do for you Soph? If I had one, that is," she asked.

I didn't have to think too long. "I would want to have all of my dreams already happening. I would want my books written, published, and to be known worldwide and to be speaking to thousands of women. That would be a good start."

"I bet a small piece of you actually wishes it were a little like that. Don't you?"

"Yeah. But I know... it's the journey and my completion of each dream which makes it all worth having." I remarked with my own bumper sticker phrase.

"Well said. Did you come up with that? Or was it something Sharesca has in her notes?"

I sat up pretending to be proud of myself. "Actually, I came up with it." I smiled at Lucy.

"That was very profound Soph. If I knew you were speaking I would buy a ticket to come hear you."

"Thanks Grandma Lucy. That means a lot to me."

"Also, you wouldn't be ready to speak to thousands of women right now. You have to warm up to that."

"True."

"Are you ready for your surprise Soph?

"Yeah I sure am. Let's do it. Will we take my car and then I can drop you back here?" I asked eagerly.

"Yes that's fine. Let me use the bathroom before we go," Lucy said as she gingerly got up from where she was sitting.

"I will clean up our tea and cookie mess and get your coat for you."

APPLE PIE WITH LUCY

11

No More Apple Pie

"Lucy? Are you there?"

Someone was holding my hand and touching the side of my face.

"No she's not Sophie. It's me, John. It's okay, I'm here."

"But... where is Grandma Lucy?" I said confused and disorientated. "Where am I?" I started to peel open my eyes but it was too bright for my eyes to handle. I opened them just enough to get a bearing on where I was.

"John?"

"Yes Sophie. It's okay. I'm here."

Why is he saying that? Where is here anyway?

"Where am I? My eyes are so heavy. And it's so bright. Why is it so bright?"

"Let me turn down the lights."

John let go of my hand. I heard what sounded like a chair being scraped across a hard floor. I tried to open my eyes again, but they refused to move much. I felt drowsy and my mind foggy.

"She's just woken up."

"Thanks for letting us know John. Is she making any sense?"

"Not a whole lot. She asked for her grandmother again. She said it's really bright in here and she is finding it hard to open her eyes."

"Okay. Let's have a look at her vitals shall we. Hi Sophie. I'm Tanya. How are you feeling?"

I was having a hard time trying to place everything together. *I just wish someone would tell me where I was. And where is Lucy?* "I'm okay. I feel sleepy. Where am I?"

"You are at St Luke's Hospital ma'am."

"What am I doing in the hospital? How did I get here?"

"It'll be okay. Just take your time. You want to go ahead and try and open your eyes up for me? Your husband John is right here. And we turned down the lights for you."

I opened my heavy eyelids slowly and readjusted to the room. John was holding my hand again. "Hey sweetie. How are you?" He was smiling at me.

"What happened to me John? Why am I in the hospital? I was just with Lucy and then I don't remember anything until now. Where are the kids? Are they okay?"

"Yes. Yes. The kids are fine. They're with Rebecca right now. She'll be bringing them by soon. You had an accident darling. You hit your head and you were out for a few days. I will let the doctor explain everything to you when she gets here, okay?"

"Out? For a few days? What day is it?"

"Don't worry sweetie. It'll be okay. The doctor will be here soon to talk to you. Everything will be fine."

"Will you stay here John? Please stay with me."

"Of course Sophie. I have been here since you arrived. I wouldn't want to be anywhere else in the world right now, but here." He was stroking the side of my face again.

"Thank you."

We both sat in silence for a while. John was being patient with me. It was lovely. It had been a long time since he had been like this.

Lucy. Did I just ask for Grandma Lucy? Did I just say I was just with her? Have I lost my mind?

"John?"

"Yes darling. What is it?" He asked concerned. Probably because I had a worried and confused look on my face.

"Did I just ask for Lucy before? And did I just say I was just with her?"

"Yes. In fact, when you were first admitted into the hospital, before you were in the coma." He stopped.

"Wait. I was in a coma? For how long?" None of this was making any sense.

"Yes you were Sophie. For three days. Before that you were in and out of consciousness and you were asking after your grandmother."

"Wow."

"Wow what?"

"I must've had the strangest dream. It all seemed so real but of course it must've been a dream."

"What did you dream about?"

"I dreamt I was with Grandma Lucy. It was as if I was *really* with her."

"Well, it must have been a dream. She passed, what, three years ago?" John smiled at me and kissed my hand. "Have some rest darling. You can tell me all about it when we get you back in good health. I bet it was a lovely dream. She was an extraordinary woman."

"Yes she was," I said smiling as I closed my eyes again and ventured back to sleep.

APPLE PIE WITH LUCY

12

Two Years from Now

After spending another week in hospital I returned home. There was some rehabilitation for another few months as I had sustained some injuries to my right knee. But, all in all, I was very lucky. The doctors said it could have been much worse. They even used the word *miracle*.

It's funny you know. I could have sworn the whole experience with my grandmother was real. Usually in my dreams I forget things that happened. Especially with time. But, not this dream. Two years later and I can still recall all of the details. Just for good measure though, about six months ago, I wrote down all the things from my 'week with Lucy'. Everything from the lessons from Sharesca, apple pie at Lucy's and the meditation room we spent so much time in. I thought it would be good to have the lessons on paper so that with time I could refer back to them.

My life looks considerably different than it did two years ago. The relationship with John has its moments, but for the most part it is pretty good. Actually, it's really good. I would give it an eight out of ten. He has a different job now. It turns out I wasn't the only one who hated the cold! And so we moved to California. I have just finished my second book which is due to come out in a week or two. My first book was not the bestseller I thought it would be. However, I know my grandmother would be quick to remind me "there is no such thing as overnight success". Hence why I haven't been called to appear on the Oprah Winfrey show yet. But, I speak regularly to women all over the US and Canada. I have also spoken in Australia and Europe. I have my own seminar company where we allow women the chance to *experience* the seven principles my grandmother taught me.

Oh! And in case you're wondering... I did find what my message for the women of the world is... *I inspire women to live a life of significance...* just like my Grandma Lucy did for me.

APPLE PIE WITH LUCY

About the Author

Melissa Aimee Haupt is the founder of *Your Dreaming Place*, a company focused on creating the space to awaken the dreamer within for women around the world. She is also a mentor, committed to providing an opportunity for women to breakthrough the limiting beliefs that are keeping them from stepping into their greatness and fulfilling their dreams.

Australia born, Melissa now resides with her husband in Scottsdale, Arizona. She is an internationally desired speaker and trainer. Her passion and mission is to see women own their greatness and to live a life of significance.

You can connect with her at:

- www.MelissaHaupt.com
- www.YourDreamingPlace.com

www.ingramcontent.com/pod-product-compliance
Lightning Source LLC
LaVergne TN
LVHW011228080426
835509LV00005B/375